WORDS on AGING

A bibliography of selected annotated references
compiled for the Administration on Aging
by the Department Library

GREENWOOD PRESS, PUBLISHERS
WESTPORT, CONNECTICUT

Library of Congress Cataloging in Publication Data

Jones, Dorothy Mounce, 1908-
   Words on aging.

   Reprint. Originally published: Washington :
U. S. Administration on Aging : for sale by the
Supt. of Docs., U.S. G.P.O., 1970 (AoA publication ;
no. 216-A)
   Includes indexes.
   1. Aged--United States--Bibliography.
2. Geriatrics--United States--Bibliography.
I. United States. Administration on Aging.
II. United States. Dept. of Health, Education,
and Welfare. Library.   III. Title.   IV. Series:
AoA publication ; no. 216-A.
Z7164.O4J58   1981 [HQ1064.U5]   016.3626   81-2471
ISBN 0-313-22860-4 (lib. bdg.)   AACR2

This is a reprint of the 1970 edition by the U.S. Department
of Health, Education and Welfare.

Reprinted in 1981 by Greenwood Press
A division of Congressional Information Service, Inc.
88 Post Road West, Westport, Connecticut 06881

Printed in the United States of America

10 9 8 7 6 5 4 3 2 1

CONTENTS

APR 15 '83

SOCIAL AND ENVIRONMENTAL SERVICES

FOREWORD

On October 6, 1969, President Nixon issued a call for a White House Conference on Aging to be held in November 1971, to consider nine major areas of need of older people: income, health, nutrition, housing, transportation, employment and retirement, education, roles and activities, and spiritual well-being.

In his call for the Conference, the President pointed out that "The entire nation and its government have increasingly recognized their responsibilty for helping older Americans to play active and constructive roles in our society. This Administration is fully committed to carrying out that responsibility . . . With careful advance planning and with broad representative participation, this Conference can help develop a more adequate national policy for Older Americans."

Much has been accomplished in recent months in providing services to older Americans and in opening opportunities to them to serve others, but much yet needs to be done. It is our intention that the 1971 White House Conference serve as a mechanism for social change, providing this national policy on aging which the President sees as so necessary.

It is our hope that this bibliography will be a useful guide for all who may be involved in the review and resolution of the problems that remain. A supplement, now in preparation, will make works of 1969 and 1970 available before the Conference is held.

JOHN B. MARTIN, *Commissioner*
Administration on Aging
Social and Rehabilitation Service

PREFACE

This, the seventh edition of selected references on aging published since 1950 (the last, 1963, was entitled *Aging in the Modern World*), like its predecessors was prepared to assist practitioners, teachers, students, and laymen working in the field of aging. There was no aim to assemble a complete bibliography on the subject but rather to provide a tool complementary to the earlier editions by listing the relevant periodical articles published from 1963 through 1967 and selected books from 1900 through 1967 with a few 1968 titles which appeared before completion of the list and seemed of primary importance. No attempt has been made to cover legislation.

To assure that no pertinent items were omitted the catalogs of the Library of Congress, the National Library of Medicine, the National Agricultural Library, the Department of Health, Education, and Welfare Library, the Department of Labor Library, the Department of Housing and Urban Development Library, and the National Institutes of Health Library, were examined.

Words on Aging was compiled at the request of the Administration on Aging by Miss Dorothy M. Jones under the direction of Mr. Charles F. Gately, Chief, Readers Services Branch. An advisory group headed by Dr. Clark Tibbitts, AoA, provided expert advice and guidance in the selection and format of the bibliography.

KANARDY L. TAYLOR, *Librarian*
Department of Health, Education, and Welfare

AGING

General Works

ALBRECHT, RUTH E., ed. Aging in a changing society. Gainesville, University of Florida Press, 1962. 187p.

Proceedings of the 11th annual Southern Conference on Gerontology. Part 1. Current concepts of aging. Part 2. Special problems related to aging. Part 3. Population changes in the past decade. Part 4. Rehabilitation factors for the aging.

ALLEGER, DANIEL E., ed. Social change and aging in the twentieth century. Gainesville, Fla., University of Florida Press, 1964. 114p.

Report of the 13th Conference on Gerontology, University of Florida.

AMERICAN MEDICAL ASSOCIATION. COMMITTEE ON AGING. Report on conferences on aging and long-term care. Chicago, 1965. 105p.

Representative selection of papers from conferences held in Oklahoma City and Chicago. Include such subjects as: home care programs, homemaker services, retirement, adult education, mental health, nursing home care, community action, health insurance, and rehabilitation.

BARRON, MILTON L. The aging American: an introduction to social gerontology and geriatrics. New York, Crowell, 1961. 269p.

Focus on retirement and the health problems of the aged in American society.

BEARD, BELLE BOONE. Social competence of centenarians. Athens, Ga., University of Georgia Printing Department, 1967. 66p.

Four papers on findings regarding the social adjustment, the social space and the level of competence of centenarians.

BEATTY, RALPH P. The senior citizen. Springfield, Ill., Thomas, 1962. 179p.

Deals with the process of aging: physical and mental problems; adaptation of older people to modern living; retirement and how to meet it; challenge of a second career.

BECHILL, WILLIAM D. Some basic priorities for services to older Americans. Washington, U.S. Govt. Print. Off., 1968. 16p. (AoA 229)

An address by the first U.S. Commissioner on Aging before the Governor's Conference on Aging, Jefferson City, Mo., October 1967.

CANADIAN CONFERENCE ON AGING. Proceedings. Ottawa, 1966. 105p.

CLARK, MARGARET, *and others.* Culture and aging; an anthropological study of older Americans. Springfield, Ill., Thomas, 1967. 478p.

Explores the aging process in the United States as shaped by the imperatives of American culture.

CONFERENCE ON LABOR. NEW YORK UNIVERSITY. Proceedings of New York University annual conference on labor. Washington, Bureau of National Affairs.

The conference is held under the auspices of the New York University Institute of Labor Relations.

COUNCIL OF STATE GOVERNMENTS. Action in the states in the field of aging, 1962–1963: a progress report. Chicago, 1964. 64p.

————. INTERSTATE CLEARING HOUSE ON MENTAL HEALTH. State units on aging; provisions for membership, officers, staffing and budgets, powers, duties and responsibilities, publications. Chicago, 1964. 58p.

DONAHUE, WILMA T., and CLARK TIBBITTS, eds. Growing in the older years. Ann Arbor, University of Michigan Press, 1951. 204p.

Emphasis of medical health, mental hygiene, and education.

———— ————. The new frontiers of aging. Ann Arbor, University of Michigan Press, 1957. 209p.

Discussions by representatives from religion, education, labor, management, government and medicine on such topics as automation, income and employment, physical and mental health, relationships with the family, and personal and social adjustment.

———— ————. Planning the older years. Ann Arbor, University of Michigan Press, 1950. 248p.

Companion volume to "Living through the older years" and organized around the three areas: living arrangements, recreational activities, and employment.

DRAKE, JOSEPH T. The aged in American society. New York, Ronald Press, 1958. 431p.

Deals with demographic characteristics of the population; employment of the aged; pension and retirement systems; physiological and psychological characteristics of the aged; and housing, recreation and educational programs for the aged.

DUKE UNIVERSITY. COUNCIL ON GERONTOLOGY. Proceedings of seminars. Durham, N.C., Regional Center for the Study of Aging.

Program and papers of the annual conference on gerontology.

DUNCAN, KENNETH J. Modern society's attitude toward aging. *Geriatrics,* v. 18, August 1963: 629–635.

Attitude is such that efforts toward improvement of the lot of the aged have good chances of success.

FEDERAL-STATE CONFERENCE ON AGING. Mobilizing resources for older people. Proceedings . . . Sponsored by Council of State Governments, Federal Council on Aging. Washington, U.S. Govt. Print. Off., 1957. 120p.

Principal addresses and reports of discussion groups.

FREEMAN, JOSEPH T., and IRVING L. WEBBER, eds. Perspectives in aging. *Gerontologist,* v. 5, March 1965: Pt. II.

Medical perspectives (12–19th century), by *Joseph T. Freeman;* biological aspects, by *Alfred H. Lawton;* human personality, by *Walter R. Miles;* social welfare aspects, by *Ollie A. Randall.*

GILBERT, JEANNE GIFFORD. Understanding old age. New York, Ronald Press, 1952. 422p.

Guide to better professional understanding of older people. Addressed particularly to psychologists, physicians, social workers, nurses, and institutional personnel.

HANSEN, GARY D., *and others.* Decade for action in gerontology and geriatric care; education-research-services-facilities, long range plan 1966–1976. Mt. Angel, Ore., Mt. Angel College, 1966. Various paging.

HANSEN, P. FROM, ed. Age with a future; proceedings of the Sixth International Congress of Gerontology, Copenhagen, 1963. Philadelphia, F. A. Davis, 1964. 662p.

HAVIGHURST, ROBERT J., and RUTH ALBRECHT. Older people. New York, Longmans, 1953. 415p.

Special problems of people as they grow old as observed in the lives of older people in a typical Midwestern American town in the middle of the 20th century.

HEYMAN, DOROTHY K., and FRANCES C. JEFFERS. Study of the relative influences of race and socio-economic status upon the activities and attitudes of a southern aged population. *Journal of Gerontology,* v. 19, April 1964: 225–229.

Differences in patterns seen to be socio-economic rather than racial.

INDUSTRIAL RELATIONS RESEARCH ASSOCIATION. The aged and society. Champaign, Ill., Twin City Printing Co., 1950. 237p.

Symposium on the problems of an aging population.

INGLEBY, BETTY, and MARGARET YORATH. Living with old age. London, Robert Hale, 1966. 233p.

Written primarily for those responsible for the care of the elderly. The question "What is old age?" is presented in Part One. Part Two deals with health aspects. Part Three is concerned with the background of work with the elderly, such as welfare services, living accommodations, and legal and financial matters.

5

JACKSON, JACQUELYNE JOHNSON. Social gerontology and the Negro: a review. *Gerontologist,* v. 7, September 1967, Pt. I: 168–178.

Impressions and conclusions concerning a collection of socio-cultural and psychological references on the Negro aged.

KASTENBAUM, ROBERT, ed. New thoughts on old age. New York, Springer, 1964. 333p.

Section I. Theoretical perspectives. Section II. Some characteristics of long-lived people. Section III. Clinical explorations. Section IV. View of old age. Section V. Organization of experience in later life.

————. Old age as a social issue. *Journal of Social Issues,* v. 21, October 1965: entire issue.

Development of research on aging; theories of human aging; psychology of aging; social adjustment in residences for the aged; government and the aging; the aged and the dying process.

KUTNER, BERNARD. Socio-economic impact of aging. *Journal of the American Geriatrics Society,* v. 14, January 1966: 33–40.

Long-range planning for the problems of aging affecting social and economic life.

LARSEN, DOROTHY HILL. Dialogues on aging. New York, Teachers College Press, 1966. 65p.

Adapted from a series of radio programs.

McFARLAND, ROSS A., *and others.* On the driving of automobiles by older people. *Journal of Gerontology.* v. 19, April 1964: 190–197.

Review of the evidence pertaining to the problem of the aging driver.

McKINNEY, JOHN C., and FRANK T. DEVYVER, eds. Aging and social policy. New York, Appleton-Century-Crofts, 1966. 338p.

Part I explores the general relationship of the aging process and the aged populace to the social, economic, and political systems of the U.S. Part II examines such critical problems as retirement, employment policy and income maintenance, housing, social services, health, and federal and state programs.

MARIN CO., CALIFORNIA. CITIZENS' ADVISORY COMMITTEE. A master plan for older adults in Marin County, California. 2d ed. San Rafael, Cal., 1965. 77p.

Preventive plans, maintenance plans, and protective and supportive plans.

MOSS, BERTRAM B., and FRASER KENT. Caring for the aged. Garden City, N.Y., Doubleday, 1966. 372p.

Practical advice for persons involved with the social, financial, medical, or psychological problems of the elderly.

6

NATIONAL CONFERENCE ON AGING. Washington, D.C. 1950. Man and his years; an account of the first national conference on aging, sponsored by the Federal Security Agency. Raleigh, N.C., Health Publications Institute, 1951. 311p.

Compilation of eleven conference section reports and a description of the conference.

NATIONAL CONFERENCE OF STATE EXECUTIVES ON AGING. Selected papers. Washington, U.S. Administration on Aging.

Published annually.

NATIONAL COUNCIL ON THE AGING. Maintaining human potential for effective and useful living; a symposium presented at the tenth anniversary meeting. . . . October 18, 1960, New York City. New York, 1961. 75p.

Includes papers on: physiological adequacy; emotional adequacy; interpersonal relationships and social adequacy; uses of leisure time; employment adequacy; and criteria of retirement.

NATIONAL OLD PEOPLE'S WELFARE COUNCIL. Annual report. London. Issued in association with the National Council of Social Service.

NATIONAL URBAN LEAGUE. Double jeopardy—the older Negro in America today. New York, 1964. 25p.

NEW YORK (STATE) LEGISLATURE. JOINT COMMITTEE ON PROBLEMS OF THE AGING. Report. Albany.

Title varies. Each report contains findings and recommendations of the committee, with papers concerning a wide range of subjects by authorities in their fields.

NUFFIELD FOUNDATION. SURVEY COMMITTEE ON THE PROBLEMS OF AGING AND THE CARE OF OLD PEOPLE. Old people. Report. London, Oxford University Press, 1947. 202p.

Report of the committee under the chairmanship of *B. Seebohm Rowntree;* surveys incomes, housing, homes and institutions, recreation, and employment.

OSTERBIND, CARTER C. Aging: a regional appraisal. Gainesville, University of Florida Press, 1961. 169p. (Institute of Gerontology series No. 10)

Report on the tenth annual Southern Conference on Gerontology held at the University of Florida, March 16–17, 1961.

Panel Discussion on Aging. *Journal of Occupational Medicine,* v. 7, October 1965: 493–501.

Economic, physiological, and psychological changes. Discussions by *Norvin C. Kiefer, Ewald W. Busse, Alvin I. Goldfarb,* and *Irving G. Roth.*

PETERSON, ROBERT. New life begins at forty. New York, Trident, 1967. 212p.

> Suggestions on diet, exercise, use of leisure time, and employment opportunities.

ROSE, ARNOLD M. Class differences among the elderly: a research report. *Sociology and Social Research,* v. 50, April 1966: 356–360.

> Notes that in relation to the lower class, the elderly middle class think themselves healthier, happier, having fewer personal problems, participating more in voluntary organizations and voting, and wishing for more religion and family life.

ROSE, ARNOLD M., and WARREN O. PETERSON, eds. Older people and their social world; the subculture of the aging. Philadelphia, F. A. Davis, 1965. 391p.

> Wide range of subject matter in social gerontology, using a variety of techniques of social research.

ROSOW, IRVING. Social integration of the aged. New York, Free Press, 1967. 354p.

> Major obstacles and opportunities that govern older people's social participation.

RUBINOW, I. M., ed. The care of the aged; proceedings of the Deutsch Foundation Conference, 1930. Chicago, University of Chicago Press, 1931. 144p. (Social service monographs, No. 14)

> The older worker in industry; state old age pensions; and the development of adequate social work for the aged.

RUDD, T. N. Professional and public attitudes to old people. *Health Education Journal,* v. 22, September 1964: 141–147.

> Unfavorable prejudices against old age are affecting geriatric work adversely.

Selected Papers from Symposium on Medical Aspects of Aging. *North Carolina Medical Journal,* v. 24, May 1963: 183–207.

> Includes articles on population, the aging skin, the aging mind, and nutrition.

SHOCK, NATHAN W. Trends in gerontology, 2d ed. Stanford, Calif., Stanford University Press, 1957. 214p.

> Review of the history of gerontological development in the following areas: the social and economic; the psychologic; the physiologic, including disease processes; and the biologic.

SIMPSON, IDA HARPER, and JOHN C. McKINNEY, eds. Social aspects of aging. Durham, N.C., Duke University Press, 1966. 341p.

> Four problem areas of social relationship of the aged: retirement, the family, the community, and perceptical life space.

SMITH, T. LYNN, ed. Living in the later years. Gainesville, University of Florida Press, 1952. 176p. (Institute of gerontology series No. 2)
Report on the second annual Southern Conference on Gerontology held at the University of Florida, January 28–29, 1952.

———. Problems of America's aging population. Gainesville, University of Florida Press, 1951. 117p. (Institute of gerontology series No. 1)
Report on the first annual Southern Conference on Gerontology held at the University of Florida, March 9–20, 1951.

Summary of Major Legislation for Older People Enacted by 89th Congress. *Aging,* No. 148, February 1967: 10–11.
Tabular presentation.

TAVES, MARVIN J., and HERMAN B. BROTMAN. Trends in public action for the aging. *Welfare in Review,* v. 3, May 1965: 1–6.
Review of recent action and pending legislation at the federal and state levels.

THUNE, JEANNE M. Racial attitudes of older adults. *Gerontologist,* September 1967, Pt. I: 179–182.
Results of a study of the racial attitudes of a large number of older adults, both Negro and white.

TIBBITTS, CLARK, ed. Handbook of social gerontology: societal aspects of aging. Chicago, University of Chicago Press. 1960. 770p.
Pt. I. Basis and theory of societal aging. Pt. II. Impact of aging on individual activities and social roles. Pt. III. Aging and the reorganization of society.

———. Living through the older years. Ann Arbor, University of Michigan Press, 1949. 193p.
Addresses delivered at the nation's first Institute on Aging, held at the University of Michigan in 1948. Lectures deal with population; maintenance of health and mental hygiene; employment; economic security; living arrangements; personal and social adjustments.

———. and JUNE L. SHMELZER. New directions in aging and their research applications. *Welfare in Review,* v. 3, February 1965: 8–14.
Recent concrete developments and new problem-solving techniques within the major action areas of aging.

———. and WILMA DONAHUE, eds. Social and psychological aspects of aging. New York, Columbia University Press, 1962. 925p. (Aging around the world, vol. 1)
Papers and abstracts from the 5th International Congress of Gerontology. Reports studies on such subjects as: population; economics of aging; housing, family and social relationships; mental health and rehabilitation; personality theory; psychology of aging.

9

TOWNSEND, PETER, and DOROTHY WEDDERBURN. The aged in the welfare state; the interim report of a survey of persons aged 65 and over in Britain, 1962 and 1963. London, G. Bell, 1965. 150p. (Occasional papers on social administration No. 14)

Survey on community care and the income and assets of older people.

U.S. ADMINISTRATION ON AGING. Designs for action for older Americans. Washington.

A series of publications reporting upon pilot research, demonstration, and training projects serving older Americans. Each with a separate title, covering a specific project or combination of projects.

————. Patterns for Progress in Aging.

A series of publications reporting in detail on a successful project for older people with sufficient information for other organizations and communities to develop a similar project adapted to their situation. Each has a specific title.

————. Federal financial assistance for projects in aging. Washington.

A series of publications describing federal agency grant programs which support projects in aging.

————. To tell the story; a public information guide for project directors. Washington, 1968. 20p.

To help directors of projects being conducted under the Older Americans Act carry out an effective and meaningful public information program.

U.S. BUREAU OF THE CENSUS. Historical statistics of the United States, colonial times to 1957. Washington, U.S. Govt. Print. Off., 1960. 789p.

Supplement to the *Statistical Abstract*, prepared with the cooperation of the Social Science Research Council.

————. Historical statistics of the United States, colonial times to 1957; continuation to 1962 and revisions. Washington, U.S. Govt. Print. Off., 1965. 154p.

————. Statistical abstract of the United States. Washington, U.S. Govt. Print. Off.

Annual summary of statistics on social, political and economic organization of the United States. Includes medical care price indexes, health and medical costs for the aged, and an extensive bibliography on statistical sources.

U.S. CONGRESS. SENATE. COMMITTEE ON LABOR AND PUBLIC WELFARE. Action for the aged and the aging. Washington, U.S. Govt. Print. Off., 1961. 303p. (86th Cong., 2nd sess., report no. 128.)

U.S. Congress. Senate. Committee on Labor and Public Welfare. The aged and aging in the United States: a national problem. A report. Washington, U.S. Govt. Print. Off., 1960. 341p. (86th Cong., 2nd sess., committee print.)

Income and health status, medical care, housing, nursing homes, social services, employment, and educational needs.

————. ————. ————. Background studies prepared by State committees for the White House Conference on Aging. A report by the Subcommittee on Problems of the Aged and Aging. Washington, U.S. Govt. Print. Off., 1960. 14 vols. (86th Cong., 2nd sess., committee print.)

————. ————. ————. Studies of the aged and the aging: selected documents. Washington, U.S. Govt. Print. Off., 1956 and 1957. 11 vols. (84th Cong., 2nd sess., committee print.)

Compilation of documents concerning the problems facing older people in America.

————. ————. ————. A survey of major problems and solutions in the field of the aged and the aging; a compilation of responses to a survey by the Subcommittee on Problems of the Aged and Aging. Washington, U.S. Govt. Print. Off., 1959. 677p. (86th Cong., 1st sess., committee print.)

————. ————. Special Committee on Aging. Developments in aging 1967. Report . . . pursuant to S. Res. 20, Feb. 17, 1967. Washington, U.S. Govt. Print. Off., 1968. 326p. (90th Cong., 2nd sess., S. rept. no. 1098.)

Resolution authorizing a study of the problems of the aged and aging

————. ————. ————. Frauds and deceptions affecting the elderly: investigations, findings, and recommendations, 1964. Washington, U.S. Govt. Print. Off., 1965. 90p. (89th Cong., 1st sess., committee print)

————. ————. ————. Major federal legislative and executive actions affecting senior citizens, 1965. Washington, U.S. Govt. Print. Off., 1965. 27p. (89th Cong., 1st sess., committee print)

Does not list bills on aging which were not reported from committees.

————. ————. ————. The 1961 White House Conference on Aging; basic policy statements and recommendations. Washington, U.S. Govt. Print. Off., 1961. 166p. (87th Cong., 1st sess., committee print)

U.S. Department of Health, Education, and Welfare. Annual report. Washington, U.S. Govt. Print. Off.

Contains report of the Secretary and reports of the operating agencies.

11

U.S. DEPARTMENT OF HEALTH, EDUCATION AND WELFARE. Grants-in-aid and other financial assistance programs administered by the U.S. Department of Health, Education, and Welfare. Washington, U.S. Govt. Print. Off.

Supplement to the "Handbook on programs of the U.S. Department of Health, Education, and Welfare."

―――. Programs and services. Washington, U.S. Govt. Print. Off., 1966. 374p.

Basic information on current HEW programs.

U.S. FEDERAL COUNCIL ON AGING. 1961 White House Conference on Aging—chart book. Aging with a future, every citizen's concern. Washington, U.S. Govt. Print. Off., 1960. 78p.

Overview of the middle-aged and older population, their financial resources, work activity, health, living arrangements, and social adjustments.

U.S. NATIONAL ADVISORY COMMITTEE FOR THE WHITE HOUSE CONFERENCE ON AGING. Background paper on Federal organizations and programs. Washington, U.S. Govt. Print. Off., 1960. 42p. (Background paper no. 20)

―――. Background paper on State organization. Washington, U.S. Govt. Print. Off., 1960. 34p. (Background paper no. 18)

U.S. PRESIDENT. Aid for the aged. Message from the President of the United States transmitting a review of measures taken to aid the older Americans and recommendations for legislation to provide further aid. Washington, U.S. Govt. Print. Off., 1967. 9p. (90th Cong., 1st sess., H. doc. no. 40)

U.S. PRESIDENT'S COUNCIL ON AGING. Annual report. Washington, U.S. Govt. Print. Off.

Each report has distinctive title. 1965–1966–1967 report has title, *A time of progress for older Americans.*

―――. On growing older. Washington, U.S. Govt. Print. Off., 1964. 146p.

"To help older people understand what happens with the passing of time and to give information that will be useful to them."

U.S. SOCIAL SECURITY ADMINISTRATION. America's centenarians. Report of interviews with social security beneficiaries who have lived to 100. Washington, 1963. 4 v.

VEDDER, CLYDE B., ed. Gerontology, a book of readings. Springfield, Ill., Thomas, 1963. 430p.

Major emphasis on sociological rather than medical or economic aspects.

VEDDER, CLYDE B., and ANNETTE S. LEFKOWITZ, comps. Problems of the aged. Springfield, Ill., Thomas, 1965. 259p.

Discussions of conditions and problems which create frustration and anxiety for older persons and how they can be remedied.

VISCHER, A. L. On growing old. Boston, Houghton, 1967. 222p.

Discusses old people in relation to their own past and to the world about them.

WEBBER, IRVING L., ed. Aging: a current appraisal. Gainesville, University of Florida Press, 1956. 179p. (Institute of Geronotology series no. 6)

Report on the sixth annual Southern Conference on Gerontology held at the University of Florida, January 19-20, 1956.

WHISKIN, FREDERICK E. The geriatric sex offender. *Geriatrics*, v. 22, October 1967: 168–172.

Examines author's reasons he considers the elderly sex offender as a maligned individual in today's society.

WHITE HOUSE CONFERENCE ON AGING. Aging in the States: a report of progress, concerns goals. Washington, U.S. Govt. Print. Off., 1961. 170p.

———. Aging with a future; a selection of papers defining goals and responsibilities for the current decade. Washington, U.S. Govt. Print. Off., 1961. 138p. (Reports and guidelines, series no. 1)

———. Federal organizations and programs in aging. Washington, U.S. Govt. Print. Off., 1961. 26p. (Reports and guidelines, series no. 13)

———. Handbook of national organizations with delegate status at the White House Conference on Aging, with plans, programs, services in the field of aging. Washington, U.S. Govt. Print. Off., 1960. 117p.

———. The Nation and its older people. Report of the White House Conference on Aging, January 9–12, 1961. Washington, U.S. Department of Health, Education, and Welfare, Special Staff on Aging, 1961. 333p.

———. Policy statement and recommendations from the White House Conference on Aging. Washington, U.S. Department of Health, Education, and Welfare, 1961. 167p.

WILLIAMS, RICHARD H., CLARK TIBBITTS, and WILMA DONAHUE, eds. Processes of aging. New York, Atherton Press, 1963. 2 vols. 1963.

Papers from an international seminar in psychosocial gerontology dealing with psychological capacities, successful aging, psychopathology of aging, relations with family and society, social factors in psychiatric disorders, and economics of health and retirement.

WOLK, ROBERT L., *and others*. The geriatric delinquent, *Journal of the American Geriatrics Society*, v. 11, July 1963: 653–659.

> Case studies of persons over 60 who committed antisocial acts within their own social milieu, but whose previous social history is devoid of such behavior.

WORKSHOP ON SOCIAL GERONTOLOGY FOR HOME ECONOMISTS, UNIVERSITY OF IOWA, 1964. Selected proceedings. Iowa City, Iowa, Dept. of Home Economics and the Institute of Gerontology, University of Iowa, 1965. 153p.

> Includes papers on: employment problems, income maintenance, psychological aspects, nutrition, leisure, housing, and education.

YOUMANS, E. GRANT, ed. Older rural Americans; a sociological perspective. Lexington, University of Kentucky Press, 1967. 321p.

> Considers older rural Americans in the contexts of work, family and the community. Analyzes the distribution of the rural aged population and their economic, housing, and health status. Treats the place and condition of older rural American Indians, Spanish-speaking people of the Southwest, and the Negro.

Population Characteristics and Forecasts

APPLEMAN, PHILIP. The silent explosion. Boston, Beacon Press, 1965. 161p.

> Problem of population growth, especially in the underdeveloped countries.

BALESTRA, PIETRO, and N. KOTESWARA RAO. Basic economic projections; United States population 1965–1980. Menlo Park, Cal., Stanford Research Institute, 1964. 70p.

> Population by state and region and by age group and sex, the birth rate, the death rate, and interstate migration.

BAYO, FRANCISCO. United States population projections for OASDHI cost estimates. Washington, U.S. Social Security Administration, Office of the Actuary, 1966. 39p. (Actuarial study no. 62)

BENJAMIN, B. Demographic and actuarial aspects of aging, with special reference to England and Wales. *Journal of the Institute of Actuaries*, v. 90, Part III, no. 386, 1964: 211–253.

> Population factors and actuarial implications of current gerontological research.

BESHERS, JAMES M. Population processes in social systems. New York, Free Press, 1967. 207p.

> Examines population processes at the societal level, and uses data referring to the individual and the family as the social unit to augment the societal measures.

BOGUE, DONALD J., ed. Applications of demography; the population situation in the U.S. in 1975. Oxford, Ohio, Scripps Foundation, 1957. 96p. (Studies in population distribution no. 13)

———. The end of the population explosion. *The Public Interest*, Spring 1967: 11–20.
   Discusses various aspects of birth control and family planning.

BRACHER, MARJORY L. SRO; overpopulation and you. Philadelphia, Fortress Press, 1966. 216p.
   Population data, determinants, and principles.

BROTMAN, HERMAN B. Profile of the older American. Washington, U.S. Govt. Print. Off., 1968. 16p. (AoA 228)
   Demographic information on the older population presented at the Conference on Consumer Problems of Older People, New York City, October 1967.

COOPER, SOPHIA, and STUART GARFINKLE. Population and labor force projections for the United States, 1960 to 1975. Washington, U.S. Govt. Print. Off., 1959. 56p. (Bureau of Labor Statistics, bulletin no. 1242)

COWLES, WYLDA B., and GORDON W. PERKINS. Planned parenthood's present and future program: our cooperative role with public health. *American Journal of Public Health*, v. 57, January 1967: 22–27.
   Description of the program of Planned Parenthood-World Population.

CUTTRELL, FLORENCE E. Older population of New York City; an analysis of the 1960 census facts. New York, Community Council of Greater New York, 1964. 172p.
   Focuses on a high proportion of those New York City families living below the "poverty line."

DAY, LINCOLN H., and ALICE TAYLOR DAY. Too many Americans. Boston, Houghton, 1964. 298p.
   Examine arguments in favor of rapid growth and expose fallacies of conservatism and religious attitudes on the question of birth control.

DUBLIN, LOUIS I. Factbook on man from birth to death. 2d ed. New York, Macmillan, 1965. 465p.
   Chapter 15. Our old people.

Factors in population growth. *Road Maps of Industry*, no. 1543, April 1, 1966: entire issue.

FORD, THOMAS R. Health and demography in Kentucky. Lexington, Ky., University of Kentucky Press, 1964. 150p.
   Drawn from 1960 U.S. census data and from local agencies.

FREEDMAN, RONALD, ed. Population: the vital revolution. Chicago, Aldine, 1964. 274p.

Non-technical survey of the most important world population trends of modern times.

GARDNER, RICHARD N. The politics of population. *Saturday Review,* v. 46, Sept. 7, 1963: 10–12; 37.

Blueprint for international family planning based on parental choice.

GOLDSCHEIDER, CALVIN. Differential residential mobility of the older population. *Journal of Gerontology,* v. 21, January 1966: 103–108.

Data on population 50 years of age or older of the adult housing unit population of the Los Angeles Standard Metropolitan Statistical Area.

HAUSER, PHILIP M. The population dilemma. Englewood Cliffs, N.J., Prentice-Hall, 1963. 188p.

Collection of papers comprising background reading for the Twenty-third American Assembly at Arden House, Harriman, N.Y., May 2–5, 1963.

HERMALIN, ALBERT I. The effect of changes in mortality rates on population growth and age distribution in the United States. *Milbank Memorial Fund quarterly,* v. 44, October 1966: 451–469.

JACOBSON, PAUL H. Cohort survival for generations since 1840. *Milbank Memorial Fund quarterly,* v. 42, July 1964, Part 1: 36–53.

Summarized under title, "Increase in survivorship since 1840," in *Statistical Bulletin, Metropolitan Life Insurance Company,* v. 45, August 1964: 1–3.

KAHN, HERMAN, and ANTHONY J. WIENER. The year 2000; a framework for speculation on the next thirty-three years. New York, Macmillan, 1967. 431p.

Statistics, projections, and information from the fields of economics, demography, history and political science, sociology, and the physical sciences.

LENZER, ANTHONY. Mobility patterns among the aged, 1955–1960. *Gerontologist,* v. 5, March 1965, Pt. I: 12–15.

Based on materials from the 1960 census of population.

MUDD, STUART, ed. The population crisis and the use of world resources. Bloomington, Ind., Indiana University Press, 1964. 562p.

Part I. The population crisis, includes articles on: the facts of population growth; economic, social and political analysis; biology and population; and action programs.

16

MURAMATSU, MINORU, and PAUL A. HARPER, eds. Population dynamics; international action and training programs. Baltimore, Johns Hopkins Press, 1965. 248p.
Proceedings of the International Conference on Population, May 1964, Johns Hopkins School of Hygiene and Public Health.

MYERS, ROBERT J. The population explosion and the United States. *Journal of the American Society of Chartered Life Underwriters,* v. 20, Winter 1966: 85-93.
Future trends in population with emphasis on changes and trends in age and sex composition.

NG, LARRY K. Y., and STUART MUDD, eds. The population crisis; implications and plans for action. Bloomington, Ind., Indiana University Press, 1965. 364p.
Condensed and reorganized version of the volume edited by Stuart Mudd, under the title *The population crisis and the use of world resources.* Some new articles have been added.

OHLIN, GORAN. Population control and economic development. Paris, Development Centre of the Organisation for Economic Co-operation and Development, 1967. 138p.
Survey, summary, and progress report on world population control.

PETERSEN, WILLIAM. Population. New York, Macmillan, 1961. 652p.
Part I. The population of the United States. Part II. Population in various types of society. Part III. The general determinants of population.

Population gains in the United States and Canada. *Statistical Bulletin, Metropolitan Life Insurance Company,* v. 48, January 1967: 3-6.
Table shows population of the U.S. by geographic area, 1957 to 1967.

The population of elders. *Statistical Bulletin Metropolitan Life Insurance Company,* v. 46, November 1965: 1-3.
Table showing population 65 and over, by sex, U.S., 1965-1985.

PRICE, DANIEL O., ed. The 99th hour; the population crisis in the United States. Chapel Hill, University of North Carolina Press, 1967. 130p.
Projections to the year 2000, criteria by which to decide what the optimum population should be, and specific steps which might be taken to reduce the rate of population growth.

Progress in longevity since 1850. *Statistical Bulletin Metropolitan Life Insurance Company,* v. 44, July 1963: 1-3.
Includes life expectancy tables, 1850-1960.

ROSSET, EDWARD. Aging process of population. New York, Macmillan, 1964. 478p.
Historical analysis of the process of the aging of the world population; translated from the Polish.

17

SHRYOCK, HENRY S., JR. Population mobility within the United States. Chicago, Community and Family Study Center, University of Chicago, 1964. 470p.

Internal migration in the United States based chiefly on data from the 1940 and 1950 census reports.

STOCKWELL, EDWARD G. Population and people. Chicago, Quadrangle, 1968. 307p.

Information on and analysis of the major elements and trends of American population.

TAEUBER, CONRAD, and IRENE B. TAEUBER. The changing population of the United States. New York, Wiley, 1958. 357p. (Census monograph series.)

Summarizes population changes of the last 100 years, including age and sex changes.

THOMLINSON, RALPH. Demographic problems; controversy over population control. Belmont, Cal., Dickenson, 1967. 117p.

Sociological analysis of selected population trends, problems, and controversies in the contemporary world, especially in the United States.

————. Population dynamics; causes and consequences of world demographic change. New York, Random House, 1965. 576p.

Analyzes causes and effects of changes in size, character, and distribution of world population.

THOMPSON, WARREN S., and DAVID T. LEWIS. Population problems. 5th ed. New York, McGraw-Hill, 1965. 593p.

Basic facts relating to population growth and changes.

UNITED NATIONS. ECONOMIC COMMISSION FOR EUROPE. Population structure in European countries. New York, 1966. 115p.

Tables and pyramids showing the distribution of population by sex, age and marital status.

U.S. ADMINISTRATION ON AGING. Facts about older Americans. Washington, U.S. Govt. Print. Off., 1966. n.p. (AoA 410)

A statistical leaflet covering number, location, income, living arrangements, marital and employment status of older people.

U.S. BUREAU OF THE CENSUS. Current population reports. Washington, U.S. Govt. Print. Off.

Issued periodically and includes population characteristics, population estimates, farm population, consumer income.

————. 1960 census of population. Washington, U.S. Govt. Print. Off.

U.S. CONGRESS. HOUSE. COMMITTEE ON THE JUDICIARY. Study of population and immigration problems. Manpower in the United States with projection to 1970. Washington, U.S. Govt. Print. Off., 1962. 31p. (Special series no. 3)

> Presentation by Dr. *Seymour L. Wolfbein,* Deputy Assistant Secretary for Employment and Manpower, U.S. Department of Labor.

U.S. NATIONAL ADVISORY COMMITTEE FOR THE WHITE HOUSE CONFERENCE ON AGING. Background paper on population trends, social and economic implications. Washington, U.S. Govt. Print. Off., 1960. 50p. (Background paper no. 1)

U.S. NATIONAL CENTER FOR HEALTH STATISTICS. Actuarial tables based on United States life tables: 1959–61. Washington, 1964. 23p. (Public health service publication no. 1252–volume 1–no. 2)

————. State life tables: 1959–61. Washington, U.S. Govt. Print. Off., 1966. 2 v. (Public Health Service publication no. 1252 volume 2– nos. 27–51)

————. United States life tables: 1959–61. Washington, 1964. 31p. (Public Health Service publication no. 1252 volume 1–no. 1)

U.S. OUTDOOR RECREATION RESOURCES REVIEW COMMISSION. Projections to the years 1976 and 2000: economic growth, labor force and leisure, and transportation. Washington, U.S. Govt. Print. Off., 1962. 434p. (ORRRC study report 23)

> Four fundamental studies which project size, distribution, income, leisure, and mobility of the American population.

VIELROSE, EGON. Elements of the natural movement of population. New York, Pergamon Press, 1965. 288p.

> Factual study of demographic phenomena against their historical backgrounds. Translated from the Polish.

WATTENBERG, BEN J., and RICHARD M. SCAMMON. This U.S.A.; an unexpected family portrait of 194,067,296 Americans drawn from the census. Garden City, N.Y., Doubleday, 1965. 520p.

> Interpretation of the statistical data in the 1960 Decennial Census.

WORLD POPULATION CONFERENCE. 2d, Belgrade, 1965. Proceedings. New York, United Nations, 1966–67. 4 v.

> Vol. 1. Summary report. Vol. 2. Fertility, family planning, mortality. Vol. 3. Projections, measurement of population trends. Vol. 4. Migration, urbanization, economic development.

Bibliographies

ADAMS, ETHEL M., and SUZANNE D. COPE, comps. Volunteers, an annotated bibliography. New York, United Community Funds and Councils of America, 1968. 26p.

> XIII. The older volunteer.

AKER, GEORGE F., comp. Adult education; procedures, methods and techniques. A classified and annotated bibliography, 1953–1963. Syracuse, N.Y., The Library of Continuing Education at Syracuse University and University College of Syracuse University, 1965. 163p.

BANEY, ANNA MAE, and ANNE B. STAGEMAN, comps. Costs of operating nursing homes and related facilities; an annotated bibliography. Washington, U.S. Public Health Service, 1959. 18p.
    Available literature on costs as distinguished from charges for care.

EDWARDS, MABEL I., comp. Selected references on home care services for the chronically ill and aged. Iowa City, Iowa, Institute of Gerontology, University of Iowa, 1967. 128p.
    Annotated bibliography.

FERGUSON, ELIZABETH. Income, resources and needs of older people; selected references, 1964. New York, National Council on the Aging, 1964. 23p.

GRAHAM, EARL C., and MARJORIE M. MULLEN, comps. Rehabilitation literature, 1950–1955; a bibliographic review of the medical care, education, employment, welfare, and psychology of handicapped children and adults. New York, McGraw-Hill, 1956. 621p.
    Supplemented by the monthly issues of *Rehabilitation Literature.*

HARPER, ERNEST B., and ARTHUR DUNHAM, eds. Community organization in action; basic literature and critical comments. New York, Association Press, 1959. 543p.
    Core of the selected materials is drawn from the literature of social work from 1900 to 1958.

HASSE, ADELAIDE R. A selected list of references on old age security. Washington, U.S. Federal Emergency Relief Administration, 1935. 4 v.
    Vol. 1. Foreign countries. Vol. 2. The United States, general and federal. Vols. 3 and 4. The states of the United States with statutory citations of laws in effect.

HAWAII UNIVERSITY. INDUSTRIAL RELATIONS CENTER. Selected readings on problems of the aged and aging; prepared for the Institute on the Older Worker, December 6, 1960. Honolulu, 1960. 55p.

Homemaker service—a bridge to the future. *Library Counselor,* v. 21, April 1966: entire issue.
    Selected annotated bibliography includes special needs of the aged and the chronically ill; with sections on casework and counseling, and recruitment and training of homemakers.

INSTITUTE OF LIFE INSURANCE AND HEALTH INSURANCE INSTITUTE. A list of worthwhile life and health insurance books. New York, 1968. 78p.
    Former editions in two separate publications, one listed health insurance books, the other life insurance books. Annotated.

Iowa University. Institute of Gerontology and Department of Home Economics. A comprehensive bibliography: the social science aspects of clothing, with implications for older women. Iowa City, State University of Iowa, 1962. 21p.

Compiled by *Mrs. Iva M. Bader,* under the direction of *Dr. Adeline M. Hoffman.*

Jones, Dorothy M. Traffic and the senior citizen; selected references. Washington, Department Library, U.S. Department of Health, Education, and Welfare, 1964. 16p. (Bibliographic series: 64-2)

Kreps, Juanita M., and Ralph Laws. Automation and the older worker; an annotated bibliography. New York, National Council on the Aging, 1963. 43p.

References analyze effect of technological advance on job opportunities, present data on age-related differences in the capacities of workers to adjust to job characteristics, and consider policy implications of automation.

———. ———. Preparation for retirement; an annotated bibliography prepared for The Committee on Employment and Retirement of the National Council on the Aging. New York, National Council on the Aging, 1965. 16p.

Morlock, Maud. Homemaker services; history and bibliography. Washington, U.S. Govt. Print. Off., 1964. 116p. (Children's Bureau publication No. 410-1964)

Muth, Lee T. A selected bibliography on the management and care of the geriatric mental patient. Washington, U.S. Bureau of Family Services, 1966. 16p.

225 references.

National Council on the Aging. Housing and living arrangements for older people: a bibliography. New York, 1967. 12p.

Odoroff, Maurice E., *and others.* Costs of operating nursing homes and related facilities; an annotated bibliography. Washington, U.S. Govt. Print. Off., 1960. 38p. (Public Health Service publication no. 754)

Princeton University. Industrial Relations Section. Current issues in federal old-age insurance. Princeton, N.J., 1967. (Selected references, no. 135)

———. ———. Organization and financing of medical care in the United States. Princeton, N.J., 1965. (Selected references, no. 123)

Psychological, physiological, health, and medical aspects of aging. *Library Counselor* (Colorado State Dept. of Public Welfare), v. 20, January 1965: entire issue.

Annotated bibliography.

References on the origin and development of social security in the United States. *Social Security Bulletin*, v. 28, August 1965: 24–26; 28; 31; 33; 36.

Rehabilitation services in public welfare. *Library counselor*, v. 18, October 1963: entire issue.
Selected annotated references.

ROSEN, GEORGE. Health is a community affair; a bookshelf compiled from the reports of the national task forces project. *American Journal of Public Health*, v. 57, April 1967: 572–583.
Sec. II. Financing community health services and facilities. Sec. IV. Health care facilities planning. Sec. V. Comprehensive health care.

SHOCK, NATHAN W. A classified bibliography of gerontology and geriatrics. Stanford, Calif., Stanford University Press, 1951. 599p.

————. Supplement 1, 1949–1955. Stanford, Calif., Stanford University Press, 1957. 525p.

————. Supplement 2, 1956–1961. Stanford, Calif., Stanford University Press, 1963. 624p.
Kept up to date with "Current publications in gerontology and geriatrics" published in each issue of *Journal of Gerontology*.

Social group work. *Library Counselor*, v. 19, October 1964: 30–42.
Bibliography.

Social services to the aging—community services in general, casework services, services in the home, services outside the home, protective services, and volunteers and friendly visiting. *Library Counselor*, v. 20, July 1965: entire issue.
Selective annotated bibliography.

The sociological aspects of aging: economic insecurity, employment, retirement planning, social relationships. housing, and recreation. *Library Counselor*, v. 20, April 1965: entire issue.
Annotated bibliography.

STAGEMAN, ANNE B. and ANNA MAE BANEY. Hospital-nursing home relationships; selected references annotated. Washington, U.S. Govt. Print. Off., 1962. 25p. (Public health service publication no. 930–G–2)

THORBY, JEAN A., and ATTWOOD, JULIA C. Public assistance medical care: an annotated bibliography, 1958–1963. Ann Arbor, Bureau of Public Health Economics, Dept. of Medical Care Organization, School of Public Health, University of Michigan, 1966. 67p.

U.S. BUREAU OF OLD-AGE AND SURVIVORS INSURANCE. Private employee benefit plans; selected annotated references (revised June 1957). Baltimore, 1957. 36p.

U.S. Dept. of Health, Education, and Welfare. Library. Aging in the modern world, an annotated bibliography. Washington, U.S. Govt. Print. Off., 1963. 194p. (OA no. 216)

Compiled for the U.S. Office of Aging. Complements earlier "Selected References on Aging." Presents annotated references to books published between 1900 and 1963, and to articles appearing from 1958 to 1963.

———. ———. Community planning for health, education, and welfare; an annotated bibliography. Washington, U.S. Govt. Print. Off., 1967. 57p.

Selections go back to 1955 articles in periodicals and to 1950 for books.

———. Office of Aging. Selected references on aging. Washington, U.S. Govt. Print. Off.

Bibliographies issued on a periodical basis, but irregularly. Each issue is on a special subject in the field of aging.

U.S. Housing and Home Finance Agency. Library. Housing for the elderly; annotated references. Washington, U.S. Govt. Print. Off., 1965. 36p.

"Most of the publications were issued since 1950. All are in the English language, but foreign techniques and developments are included."

U.S. Library of Congress. Division of Bibliography. Select list of references on old age and civil service pensions. Washington, U.S. Govt. Print. Off., 1903. 18p.

Supplement issued in 1912.

———. Legislative Reference Service. Selected list of publications of the committees of the Congress relating to health, medical care, medical facilities, and rehabilitation. Washington, U.S. Govt. Print. Off., 1961. 71p.

Listed both by committee and by subject. Arranged by year with most recent entries first.

U.S. National Library of Medicine. Physiologic involution in normal aging man; a bibliography of literature 1956–1960. Washington, 1960. 29p.

U.S. Public Health Service. Nursing care of the aged; an annotated bibliography for nurses. Washington, U.S. Govt. Print. Off., 1967. 131p. (Public Health Service publication no. 1603)

Covers the period 1954–65.

———. Nursing homes; an annotated reading list. Washington, U.S. Govt. Print. Off., 1962. 46p. (Public Health Service publication no. 907)

Representative articles published in the 5-year period, 1956–1960.

U.S. PUBLIC HEALTH SERVICE. Nutrition and food service in nursing homes and homes for the aged; selected references. Washington, U.S. Govt. Print. Off., 1960. 11p. (Public Health Service publication no. 786, bibliography series no. 31.)

———. DIVISION OF HOSPITAL AND MEDICAL FACILITIES. Selected references relating to administration and operation of nursing homes and related facilities. Washington, 1960.

U.S. SOCIAL SECURITY ADMINISTRATION. Basic readings in social security. Compiled for the Social Security Administration by the Library of the U.S. Department of Health, Education, and Welfare. Washington, U.S. Govt. Print. Off., 1960. 221p. (Publication no. 28, 1960)
Annotated bibliography of significant books, pamphlets, and articles on the Social Security Act and programs administered.

———. LIBRARY. Medicare; a bibliography of selected references, 1966/ 1967. Washington, U.S. Govt. Print. Off., 1968. 88p.
Significant books, pamphlets and journal articles added to the Social Security Administration Library during the year, July 1, 1966–June 30, 1967.

———. ———. Selected current references on the medicare program. Baltimore, 1966. 50p.

U.S. VETERANS ADMINISTRATION. MEDICAL AND GENERAL REFERENCE LIBRARY. Nursing home care, a bibliography 1953–1963. Washington, 1964. 40p.

WARD, BETTY ARNETT. Education on the aging; a selected annotated bibliography. Washington, U.S. Govt. Print. Off., 1958. 145p. (U.S. Office of Education Bulletin (1958) no. 11)

WILKINSON, ANN M. Administration of long-term care institutions; guide to information sources. Ithaca, N.Y., Cornell University, Graduate School of Business and Public Administration, 1967. 45p. (Bibliography series no. 3)

PROCESSES of AGING

Biological Aging

Advances in gerontological research. New York, Academic Press. Series of volumes started in 1964, which contain collections of articles on topics of potential fundamental significance to the aging process.

AGATE, JOHN. The practice of geriatrics. Springfield, Ill., Thomas, 1963. 490p.
   "Shows how in senescence the natural history of disease may take unexpected turns, and it gives particular attention to the hazards of being both old and ill together."

BALKE, BRUNO. Experimental evaluation of work capacity as related to chronological and physiological aging. Oklahoma City, Okla., U.S. Federal Aviation Agency, Aviation Medical Service, Aeromedical Research Division, Civil Aeromedical Research Institute, 1963. 6p.

BIRREN, JAMES E., comp. Relations of development and aging; a symposium presented before the Gerontological Society at the 15th annual meeting. . . . Springfield, Ill., Thomas, 1964. 296p.
   Section A. Background. Section B. Biological manifestations of growth and aging. Section C. Changes in psychological functions. Section D. Personality and social processes.

———, and others, eds. Human aging; a biological and behavioral ~udy. Washington, U.S. Govt. Print. Off., 1963. 328p. (Public Health ~ice publication, no. 986)
   ~ve analysis by 22 investigators at the National Institute of ~alth on the psychiatric, psychological, physiological, ~ psychological characteristics of 47 optimally healthy ~65 to 91 years of age.

BR~, AUSTIN M., and GEORGE A. SACHER, eds. Aging and levels of biological organization. Chicago, University of Chicago Press, 1965. 353p.
   Proceedings of a conference, sponsored by the American Institute of Biological Sciences, at which the participants examined the problem of metazoan aging at all levels of organization, ranging from molecules and cells to ecosystems.

BURNIGHT, ROBERT G. Chronic morbidity and the socio-economic characteristics of older urban males. *Milbank Memorial Fund Quarterly*, v. 43, July 1965: 311–322.
   Investigates changes which occur in health characteristics in the seventh decade of life.

CANDER, LEON, and JOHN H. MOYER, eds. Aging of the lung; perspectives. The tenth Hahnemann symposium. New York, Grune, 1964. 371p.

COLE, MILTON B., and OKSANA LYCZKOWSKJ. Some characteristics of a group of senior citizen volunteers for physiological studies. *Journal of the American Geriatrics Society,* v. 15, January 1967: 82–86.
Findings from heat tolerance workload studies.

COMFORT, ALEX. Aging; the biology of senescence. Rev. ed. New York, Holt. 365p.

CONFERENCE OF PROBLEMS OF AGING. Transactions of the annual conference. New York, Josiah Macy, Jr. Foundation, 1938–1954.
Conferences sponsored by Josiah Macy, Jr. Foundation. First conference transactions edited by Dr. E. V. Cowdry entitled "Problems of aging, biological and medical aspects."

COWDRY, EDMUND VINCENT, ed. Problems of aging, biological and medical aspects. 3rd ed. Baltimore, Williams and Wilkins, 1952. 1061p.
New edition edited by A. I. Lansing brings together recent accounts of biological and medical aspects of the problem, together with a number of sociological and economical contributions.

CURTIS, HOWARD J. Biological mechanisms of aging. Springfield, Ill., Thomas, 1966. 133p.
Examines the many theories of aging in the light of modern biological concepts.

DALDERUP, LOUISE M., *and others.* Basal metabolic rate, anthropometric, electrocardiographic, and dietary data relating to elderly persons. *Journal of Gerontology,* v. 21, January 1966: 22–26.
Physiological measurements in a group of elderly men and wom

DE ROPP, ROBERT S. Man against aging. New York, St
1960. 310p.
A biochemist traces man's struggle against the ag
the earliest times to the latest scientific discoveries.

DUNBAR, FLANDERS. Emotions and bodily changes; a survey of literature on psychosomatic interrelationships, 1910–1953. 4th ed. New York, Columbia University Press, 1954. 1192p.
"Each major topic represents a written chapter and a bibliographical list. The written chapters are made up of abstracts of parts or the whole of such articles in the list as contain a definite contribution, positive or negative, to our problem."

ENGLE, EARL T., and GREGORY PINCUS, eds. Hormones and the aging process. New York, Academic Press, 1956. 323p.
Proceedings of a conference held at Arden House, Harriman, New York, 1955.

FREEMAN, JOSEPH T., ed. Clinical features of the older patient. Springfield, Ill., Thomas, 1965. 491p.

Outlines interrelated morphological, physiological and adaptive natures of mechanisms whose goals are altered during senescence.

GITMAN, LEO, comp. Endocrines and aging. Springfield, Ill., Thomas, 1967. 305p.

Symposium presented before the 17th annual meeting of the Gerontological Society.

GRANT, RICHARD L. Concepts of aging: an historical review. *Perspectives in Biology and Medicine*, v. 6, Summer 1963: 443–478.

Discusses various theories on the causes of aging.

HALL, DAVID A. Elastolysis and aging. Springfield, Ill., Thomas, 1964. 160p.

The substrate and the enzyme systems which act on it, and the possible implications of the interaction between them in the phenomena of aging in elastic tissue.

KIEFER, NORVIN C., and MANUEL RODSTEIN. Aging—facts and fallacies. *Sight-Saving Review*, v. 35, Summer 1965: 68–74.

"Correlation of physiological age of body and mind with chronological age can be expressed only in terms of a range so extremely wide that frequently it has little reliable usefulness."

KROHN, PETER L., ed. Topics in the biology of aging; a symposium held at the Salk Institute for Biological Studies. . . . New York, Interscience, 1966. 177p.

Papers examining and evaluating some of the most recent work on the biology of aging.

McCLELLAN, WALTER S. Physical medicine and rehabilitation for the aged. Springfield, Ill., Thomas, 1951. 81p.

Discusses physiologic changes in the aged which influence response to treatment. Deals briefly with rehabilitation and occupational therapy.

McKEOWN, FLORENCE. Pathology of the aged. London, Butterworth, 1965. 361p.

Special emphasis on the major disorders such as cardiovascular disease, malignancy and disturbances of the nervous system.

MARXER, WEBSTER L., and GEORGE R. COWGILL, eds. The art of predictive medicine; the early detection of deteriorative trends. Springfield, Ill., Thomas, 1967. 358p.

MONTAGNA, WILLIAM, ed. Aging; proceedings of the symposium held at the University of Oregon Medical School, 1964. New York, Pergamon Press, 1965. 273p. (Advances in biology of skin, v. VI.)

Morphology, biochemistry and physiology of aging skin.

Rubin, Isadore. Sexual life after sixty. New York, Basic Books, 1965. 274p.

Samis, Harvey V., Jr., ed. A symposium on the role of biological information systems in development and aging. *Journal of Gerontology*, v. 22, October 1967: Part II.

"A consensus has emerged from this group of papers. It is that the state of a biological unit depends not only on the fidelity with which gene-based information is translated into form and function but, equally, upon the systems which control the translation."

Shock, Nathan W., ed. Aging—some social and biological aspects. Symposia presented at the Chicago meeting of the American Association for the Advancement of Science, December 29-30, 1959. Washington, 1960. 427p. (American Association for the Advancement of Science, publication no. 65)

————. Biological aspects of aging. New York, Columbia University Press, 1962. 391p. (Aging around the world, vol. 3)

Proceedings of the fifth Congress of the International Association of Gerontology. Basic biological problems of aging.

————. Current trends in research on the physiological aspects of aging. *Journal of the American Geriatrics Society*, v. 15, November 1967: 995-1000.

————, comp. and ed. Perspectives in experimental gerontology; a festschrift for Dr. F. Verzar. Springfield, Ill., Thomas, 1966. 409p.

Overview of ideas and projection of future developments in the field of experimental gerontology.

Stieglitz, Edward J. The second 40 years. Philadelphia, Lippincott, 1952. 317p.

Describes what happens to the body and the mind during the process of aging.

Strehler, Bernard L. Time, cells, and aging. New York, Academic Press, 1962. 270p.

Analyzes and reviews recent findings in the biology of aging in the context of earlier knowledge.

————. *and others*, eds. The biology of aging; a symposium held at Gatlinburg, Tenn., May 1-3, 1957, under the sponsorship of the AIBS and with support of the National Science Foundation. Washington, American Institute of Biological Sciences, 1960. 364p. (Publication no. 6)

U.S. National Advisory Committee for the White House Conference on Aging. Background paper on research in gerontology: biological. Washington, U.S. Govt. Print. Off., 1960. 41p. (Background paper no. 14)

WEALE, ROBERT A. The aging eye. New York, Harper, 1963. 200p.
Broad survey of the field.

WESSEL, JANET A., *and others*. Functional responses to submaximal exercise in women 20–69 years. *Journal of Gerontology*, v. 21, April 1966: 168–181.
Study to determine the energy metabolism and related responses during and after a submaximal work load and their relationship to age.

WHITE HOUSE CONFERENCE ON AGING. Research in gerontology: biological and medical. Washington, U.S. Govt. Print. Off., 1961. 127p. (Reports and guidelines, series no. 10)

Mental Health and Illness

ASSOCIATION FOR RESEARCH IN NERVOUS AND MENTAL DISEASE. The neurologic and psychiatric aspects of the disorders of aging; proceedings of the association, December 9 and 10, 1955, New York, N.Y. Baltimore, Williams and Wilkins, 1956. 307p.

BARTON, WALTER E. Administration in psychiatry. Springfield, Ill., Thomas, 1962. 773p.
Chapter V. Treatment of the aged patient.

BEREZIN, MARTIN A., and STANLEY H. CATH, eds. Geriatric psychiatry: grief, loss, and emotional disorders in the aging process. New York, International Universities Press, 1965. 380p.
Papers from two symposia arranged by the Boston Society for Gerontologic Psychiatry.

COHEN, ELIAS S. Nursing homes, state hospitals, and the aged mentally ill. *Geriatrics*, v. 18, November 1963: 871–876.
Relationship of state mental hospitals and nursing homes to potential patients.

CONFER, CHARLES E., and L. RICHARD LESSOR. Preventive mental health groups for the aged. *Lutheran Social Welfare Quarterly*, v. 1, Summer 1967: 44–54.
Program conceived, planned, and carried out by a social agency in cooperation with a group of congregations.

CONFERENCE ON MENTAL IMPAIRMENT IN THE AGING. A community looks at its practices for improving services to the mentally impaired aging; proceedings . . . New York, Central Bureau for the Jewish Aged, 1965. 48p.

FRIEDMAN, JACOB H., and DAVID M. BRESSLER. A geriatric mental hygiene clinic in a general hospital: first two years of operation. *Journal of the American Geriatrics Society,* v. 12, January 1964: 71–78.

Describes program and operation of the first clinic of its type connected with a general hospital in the United States.

GOLDFARB, ALVIN I. The psychiatric aspects of aging. *New York medicine,* v. 22, October 20, 1966: 562–564.

Directed to the physician in private practice.

———. Psychiatry in geriatrics. *Medical Clinics of North America,* v. 51, November 1967: 1515–1527.

The physician's role in the care of the aged mentally disordered person.

———, *and others.* Predictors of mortality in the institutionalized aged. *Diseases of the Nervous System,* v. 27, January 1966: 21–29.

Report on the mortality within one year of a representative institutionalized sample of aged persons.

GROUP FOR THE ADVANCEMENT OF PSYCHIATRY. COMMITTEE ON AGING. Psychiatry and the aged: an introductory approach. New York, 1965: 527–574. (Report no. 59)

HANDY, IMENA A. The geriatric psychiatric patient—a challenge for social workers. *Journal of the American Geriatrics Society,* v. 14, October 1966: 1067–1071.

Outlines reasons for the reluctance of social workers to deal with geriatric psychiatric patients.

HANSEN, A. VICTOR, JR. The management of the senile patient. *Pennsylvania Medical Journal,* v. 67, May 1964: 32–34.

A proposed plan to permit an agency or individual to assume responsibility and management of an incompetent older person who has no family and limited means.

HOCH, PAUL H., and JOSEPH ZUBIN, eds. The evaluation of psychiatric treatment. New York, Grune, 1964. 326 p.

The evaluation of geriatric patients following treatment, by *Alvin I. Goldfarb.*

INSTITUTE ON MENTALLY IMPAIRED AGED. Mental impairment in the aged. Philadelphia, Philadelphia Geriatric Center, 1965. 176p.

Definition of the problem of mental impairment, social research in this area, and treatment and planning.

JAMES, GEORGE. Mental health services for older people. *Geriatrics,* v. 22, May 1967: 162–167.

Explores approaches to getting the right care to the aged mentally ill patient.

KAPLAN, OSCAR J., ed. Mental disorders in later life. 2d ed., Stanford University Press, 1956. 508p.

Collection of essays selected to indicate the level of achievement in the area of mental diseases in later life.

KLEIN, WILMA H., and others. Promoting mental health of older people through group methods; a practical guide. New York, Mental Health Materials Center, 1965. 156p.

KRAL, V. A. Psychiatric aspects of aging. *Canadian Medical Association Journal,* v. 93, October 9, 1965: 792–796.

Psychodynamic factors and their interplay are responsible for the neurotic conditions of the elderly.

KRAUSS, THEODORE C., and HENRY N. GOLDSTEIN. Medical management of mentally impaired patients in long-term care facilities. *Gerontologist,* v. 7, December 1967: 278–282.

Discussion of experiences at the Rosa Coplon Jewish Home and Infirmary, Buffalo, N.Y.

LANDSMAN, GEORGE. Explorations in mental health programs for the aging. *Gerontologist,* v. 3, September 1963: 105–109.

Reviews programs supported by grants from the National Institute of Mental Health.

LOCKE, NORMAN. Strengthening mental health services to the aging. *Geriatrics,* v. 21, September 1966: 201–204.

More understanding care by day center staff members can result from professional consultation with the staff.

LOWENTHAL, MARJORIE FISKE, and others. Aging and mental disorders in San Francisco; a social psychiatric study. San Francisco, Jossey-Bass, 1967. 341p.

Group of distressed non-institutionalized persons over 60 compared with several hundred similar people who became institutionalized for mental illness.

MASON, AARON S. The hospital service clinic—a work modality for the geriatric mental patient. *Journal of the American Geriatrics Society,* v. 13, June 1965: 545–549.

Hospital service clinic in the VA Hospital at Tomah, Wisconsin to afford the male geriatric patient an opportunity to perform socially useful work.

MENSH, IVAN NORMAN. Studies of older psychiatric patients. *Gerontologist,* v. 3, September 1963: 100–104.

Review of British and American studies.

MT. ANGEL COLLEGE. OREGON GERONTOLOGY STUDY AND TRAINING CENTER. Mental health and aging in Oregon. Mt. Angel, Ore., 1965. 71p.

Guidelines for a long-range program in mental health for older persons.

Panel discussion—psychiatric aspects of geriatric patients. *Journal of the American Geriatrics Society*, v. 13, February 1965: 108–117.

> The neurology and psychiatry of old age, by *George N. Thompson*. Social and related factors leading to psychiatric hospitalization of the aged, by *Marjorie Fiske Lowenthal*. A comparative study of the neuropathologic findings in senile psychoses and in "normal senility," by *N. Malamud*.

PEMBERTON, ANNIE MAY. Helping other people who have been in mental hospitals. Chicago, American Public Welfare Association, 1954. 16p. (How public welfare serves aging people, no. 2)

POST, FELIX. Persistent persecutory states of the elderly. New York, Pergamon Press, 1966. 100p.

> Reviews literature on late schizophrenia and describes personal experiences with some 100 patients.

RIPPETO, ROBERT D. The disability of senility. *Geriatrics*, v. 21, February 1966: 205–214.

> Concentrates on senility resulting from life patterns of earlier years and describes nursing home procedures in the care of the senile.

SCHWARTZBERG, ALLAN Z. The older psychiatric patient and the community. *Geriatrics*, v. 22, April 1967: 182–186.

> Rehabilitation depends on comprehensive diagnosis coupled with major attention to the patient's family by the physician and the caseworker.

STERN, EDITH M. Mental illness; a guide for the family. New York, Harper, 1962. 127p.

> Practical explanation of the problems confronting relatives of the mentally ill.

TIMM, OREON K. Modern trends in psychiatric care of the geriatric patient. *Journal of the American Geriatrics Society*, v. 13, December 1965: 1025–1031.

> Discusses a comprehensive psychiatric program for geriatric patients.

TURNER, HELEN, ed. A psychiatric approach to institutional work with the aged. New York, Community Service Society, 1955.

> Minutes of a psychiatric seminar conducted by Dr. Alvin I. Goldfarb for the staff of the Study Project in Services for the Aging, Community Service Society of New York.

U.S. NATIONAL CLEARINGHOUSE FOR MENTAL HEALTH INFORMATION. Research utilization in aging, an exploration. Washington, U.S. Govt. Print. Off., 1964. 117p. (Public Health Service publication no. 1211)

> Principles, problems, methods, and means of implementing research findings for the aging in mental health program planning and development.

U.S. PUBLIC HEALTH SERVICE. Mental disorders of the aging. Washington, U.S. Govt. Print. Off., 1963. 19p. (Public Health Service publication no. 993)

Briefly discusses mental disorders of the aged and their treatment.

WEIL, JULIUS. Special program for the senile in a home for the aged. *Geriatrics*, v. 21, January 1966: 197-202.

Describes project of the Montefiore Home in Cleveland Heights, Ohio, to provide senile and slightly mentally confused older people with a protective setting.

WOLFF, KURT. The confused geriatric patient. *Journal of the American Geriatrics Society*, v. 12, March 1964: 266-270.

Discusses treatment of patients suffering from acute or chronic brain syndrome due to cerebral arteriosclerosis or senility.

————. The elder patient, psychiatric disorders and their management. *Journal of the American Geriatrics Society*, v. 15, June 1967: 575-586.

Discusses present treatment methods and the biological, sociological, and psychological needs of the geriatric patient which must be understood and treated accordingly.

WOLK, ROBERT L., and ALVIN I. GOLDFARB. The response to group psychotherapy of aged recent admissions compared with long-term mental hospital patients. *American Journal of Psychiatry*, v. 123, April 1967: 1251-1257.

Physical Health and Illness

Accidental injury and death at the older ages. *Statistical Bulletin Metropolitan Life Insurance Co.*, v. 46, February 1965: 6-8.

AMERICAN MEDICAL ASSOCIATION. COMMITTEE ON AGING. Health aspects of aging. Chicago, 1965. 70p.

AMERICAN PUBLIC HEALTH ASSOCIATION. PROGRAM AREA COMMITTEE ON ACCIDENT PREVENTION. Accident prevention; the role of physicians and public health workers. New York, McGraw-Hill, 1961. 400p.

Chapter 6. "Accidents to the Aged," by *A. L. Chapman.*

ANDERSON, W. FERGUSON. Practical management of the elderly. Philadelphia, F. A. Davis, 1967. 304p.

Guide for the doctor interested in his elderly patients, with no attempt to discuss in detail the symptoms and signs of disease.

BICK, EDGAR MILTON. Trauma in the aged. New York, McGraw-Hill, 1960. 524p.

BLUMENTHAL, HERMAN T., ed. Medical and clinical aspects of aging. New York, Columbia University Press, 1962. 690p.

Appearance and nature of clinical diseases in old age. Proceedings of the Fifth Congress of the International Association of Gerontology.

BOYLE, ROBERT W., and MICHAEL REID. What happens to the stroke victim? *Geriatrics,* v. 20, November 1965: 949–955.

Study shows mortality in geriatric stroke patients following hospital discharge is high.

CARTER, HOWARD W., *and others.* The aged and chronic disease; research in a local health department. Jacksonville, Fla., Florida State Board of Health, 1966. 243p. (Monograph series no. 9)

COE, RODNEY M. Professional perspectives on the aged. *Gerontologist,* v. 7, June 1967, Pt. I: 114–119.

Describes the therapist-patient encounter.

COMMISSION ON CHRONIC ILLNESS. Chronic illness in the United States. Cambridge, Harvard University Press, 1957. 4 v.

Vol. I. Prevention of chronic illness. Vol. II. Care of the long-term patient. Vol. III. Chronic illness in a rural area. Vol. IV. Chronic illness in a large city, the Baltimore study.

CONFERENCE ON MEDICINE IN OLD AGE. Proceedings. Philadelphia, Lippincott, 1966. 226p.

Papers presented at a conference held at the Royal College of Physicians of London on the 18th and 19th of June 1965.

CONFERENCE ON THE GERIATRIC AMPUTEE. The geriatric amputee; a report on a conference sponsored by the Committee on Prosthetics Research and Development of the Division of Engineering and Industrial Research. Washington, National Academy of Sciences-National Research Council, 1961. 245p. (National Research Council publication no. 919)

COWDRY, E. V., ed. The care of the geriatric patient. 3d ed. St. Louis, Mosby, 1968. 430p.

The approach to the subject matter in this edition is strictly clinical.

DASCO, MICHAEL M. Restorative medicine in geriatrics. Springfield, Ill., Thomas, 1963. 324p.

Deals with the active clinical care of the elderly disabled.

FIELD, MINNA. Patients are people; a medical-social approach to prolonged illness. 3rd ed. New York, Columbia University Press, 1967. 294p.

FREEMAN, JOSEPH T., ed. Clinical principles and drugs in the aging. Springfield, Ill., Thomas, 1963. 485p.

Colloquium dealing with pharmacological aspects of aging.

GERONTOLOGICAL SOCIETY. Working with older people; a guide to practice. Vol. 1: The practitioner and the elderly. Washington, U.S. Govt. Print. Off., 1967. 52p. (Public Health Service publication no. 1459, Vol. 1)

Aimed at helping the practitioner understand the elderly person and provides background on health maintenance for the elderly with guidelines for planning community health services.

GLENN, FRANK, and others, eds. Surgery in the aged. New York, McGraw-Hill, 1960. 534p.

Prepared by the New York Hospital-Cornell Medical College Surgical Staff.

GRAY, ROBERT MACK, and others. Stress and health in later maturity. Journal of Gerontology, v. 20, January 1965: 65–68.

Assesses the relationship between stress and medical health of elderly persons.

GRIFFITH, GEORGE C. Home care of the aged cardiac patient. Geriatrics, v. 22, June 1967: 140–143.

Approach based on the care of the patient rather than the disease.

HAZELL, KENNETH. Elderly patients; their medical care before and after operation. Springfield, Ill., Thomas, 1962. 191p.

———. Social and medical problems of the elderly. 2d ed. Springfield, Ill., Thomas, 1966. 272p.

Main emphasis on the technical aspects of medical care within the social framework of the problem. New edition contains chapters by Russell Barton on medical disorders, and by W. Ferguson Anderson on preventive medicine.

HUMPHRIES, M. K., JR. Eye problems of the elderly, cause and treatment. Virginia Medical Monthly, v. 92, November 1965: 520–526.

HURWITZ, ARCHIE R. Dentomedical problems of the geriatric patient. Geriatrics, v. 21, September 1966: 133–138.

Discusses cooperative dental-medical management and treatment.

JESSEPH, JOHN E., and HENRY N. HARKINS. Geriatric surgical emergencies. Boston, Little, 1963. 447p.

Eighteen specialists from the University of Washington School of Medicine give step-by-step advice on methods of detecting and handling conditions with related complications.

37

JOHNSON, WINGATE M., ed. The older patient. New York, Hoeber, 1960. 589p.

Ranges "From the how and why of the physical examination over the broad area of medical specialties, ending with comments on adjustment to old age."

KNOWLES, LOIS N., ed. Maintaining high level wellness in older years. Gainesville, University of Florida Press, 1965. 97p. (Institute of Gerontology series, v. 14)

Report on the 14th annual Southern Conference on Gerontology held at the University of Florida, February 15-16, 1965.

KORNZWEIG, A. L. Eye health needs of persons in an institution for the aged. *Sight-Saving Review,* v. 34, Summer 1964: 83-87.

Describes an eye clinic at the Jewish Home and Hospital for Aged of New York City.

LAWTON, M. POWELL, *and others.* Indices of health in an aging population. *Journal of Gerontology,* v. 22, July 1967: 334-342.

Factor analytic approach to define dimensions of health among older men and women assumes that health is a multidimensional attribute, rather than a unitary state.

LILIENFELD, ABRAHAM M., *and others,* eds. Chronic diseases and public health. Baltimore, Johns Hopkins Press, 1966. 846p.

Includes chapters on the care of the long-term patient and economic aspects of long-term illness.

LOKSHIN, HELEN. Helping the aged person with medical decision at point of crisis. *Journal of Jewish Communal Service,* v. 41, Summer 1965: 393-401.

Case studies with suggestions for services needed.

LORHAN, PAUL H. Geriatric anesthesia. Springfield, Ill., Thomas, 1955. 90p.

MACLACHLAN, JOHN M., ed. Health in the later years. Gainesville, University of Florida Press, 1953. 123p. (Institute of Gerontology series no. 3)

Report on the third annual Southern Conference on Gerontology held at the University of Florida, January 26-27, 1953.

MARTIN, JOHN, and ANN DORAN. Evidence concerning the relationship between health and retirement. *Sociological Review,* n. s., v. 14, November 1966: 329-343.

Analyzes survey data concerning the incidence of serious illness before and after retirement.

MITTY, WILLIAM F., JR. Surgery in the aged; seventy-five years of age and over. Springfield, Ill., Thomas, 1966. 110p.

Detailed outline of operative techniques and principles of surgery.

Moss, Bertram B. Emotional problems of the aged and those who care for them. *Journal of the American Geriatrics Society*, v. 13, August 1965: 348–354.

Discusses the role of the physician of the aged and terminally ill and his relationship to the patient and the patient's family.

Myers, J. Arthur. Chronic pulmonary tuberculosis among persons in the upper age brackets. *Geriatrics*, v. 20, May 1965: 402–412.

Elderly persons in the community constitute a seedbed of tubercle bacilli without adequate management.

Post, Felix. The significance of effective symptoms in old age; a follow-up study of one hundred patients. London, Oxford University Press, 1962. 106p. (Institute of Psychiatry, Maudsley monographs, no. 10)

Retirement Council. Better health after fifty. New York, 1964. 128p. Guide to the habits of healthful living.

Rippeto, Robert D. Social disabilities created by gait disturbances in the aged. *Geriatrics*, v. 22, April 1967: 175–181.

Emphasis on gait disorders in terms of employment, housing requirements, recreation, and reaction to community attitudes.

Rodstein, Manuel. Accidents among the aged: incidence, causes and prevention. *Journal of Chronic Diseases*, v. 17, June 1964: 515–526.

Rogot, Eugene. Survivorship among the aged blind. *New Outlook for the Blind*, v. 59, December 1965: 333–338.

Based on statistics from a statewide register of the blind maintained by the Massachusetts Division of the Blind.

Rothenberg, Robert E. Health in the later years. New York, New American Library, 1964. 702p.

Medical guide using direct question-and-answer method.

Saussele, Herman P. Health and vigor after fifty. New York, Vantage, 1965. 202p.

Nutrition, exercise, sleep, and other guides to health.

Shanas, Ethel. The health of older people; a social survey. Cambridge, Harvard University Press, 1962. 250p.

Summary of the findings of a 1957 survey on the health needs of older people as reported in a nationwide sample of persons 65 years and over. It includes employment, families, income, living arrangements, and medical care.

Silverman, Betsy Marden, ed. Positive health of older people. New York, National Health Council, 1960. 131p.

Based on discussions at the 1960 National Health Forum.

U.S. Administration on Aging. The fitness challenge in the later years. Washington, U.S. Govt. Print. Off., 1968. 28p.

An exercise program for older people, developed in cooperation with the President's Council on Physical Fitness and Sports.

U.S. National Center for Health Statistics. Characteristics of persons with impaired hearing, United States—July 1962–June 1963. Washington, U.S. Govt. Print. Off., 1967. 64p. (Public Health Service publication no. 1000, series 10, no. 35)

Demographic and other characteristics of persons with a binaural hearing impairment, classified according to amount of hearing loss.

―――. Chronic illness among residents of nursing and personal care homes: United States, May–June 1964. Washington, U.S. Govt. Print. Off., 1967. 43p. (Public Health Service publication no. 1000, series 12, no. 7)

Health status of residents of nursing and personal care homes as reflected by the number of chronic ailments reported.

―――. Episodes and duration of hospitalization in the last year of life, United States—1961. Washington, U.S. Govt. Print. Off., 1966. 48p. (Public Health Service publication no. 1000, series 22, no. 2)

Statistics by age, sex, color, residence, and cause of death.

―――. Health characteristics by geographic region, large metropolitan areas, and other places of residence; United States, July 1963–June 1965. Washington, U.S. Govt. Print. Off., 1967. 58p. (Public Health Service publication no. 1000, series 10, no. 36)

Statistics on chronic activity limitation, disability, days, persons injured, acute condition, short-stay hospital discharges, physician and dental visits, by age and geographic region.

―――. Selected family characteristics and health measures reported in the health interview survey. Washington, U.S. Govt. Print. Off., 1967. 26p. (Public Health Service publication no. 1000, series 3, no. 7)

Standardized morbidity ratios for measures of illness by family size, family type, and family income.

U.S. President's Commission on Heart Disease, Cancer and Stroke. A national program to conquer heart disease, cancer and stroke; report. Washington, U.S. Govt. Print. Off., 1964–65. 2 v.

Vol. I. Summary. Vol. II. Full reports of 8 subcommittees and additional scientific and technical documentation.

U.S. Public Health Service. Office evaluation of the aging patient; disease detection in persons over 45. Washington, U.S. Govt. Print. Off., 1966. n.p. (Public Health Service publication no. 1513)

Graphic presentation of office procedures in disease detection.

WASSERSUG, JOSEPH D. How to be healthy and happy after sixty. New York, Abelard-Schuman, 1966. 176p.

In popular terms, discusses how the mind and body grow old and how to keep them young.

WEBBER, IRVING L., ed. Society and the health of older people. Gainesville, University of Florida Press, 1959. 153p. (Institute of Gerontology series no. 9)

Report on the ninth annual Southern Conference on Gerontology held at the University of Florida, March 19-20, 1959.

WILBAR, CHARLES L. Health aspects of the driver licensure program of Pennsylvania. *American Journal of Public Health,* v. 55, November 1965: 1807-1812.

Emphasis on the role an examination program can play.

YOUMANS, E. GRANT. Health orientations of older rural and urban men. *Geriatrics,* v. 22, October 1967: 139-147.

Compares views on health of two age groups of men, 60 to 64 and 75 and over, living in different environments.

ZONNEVELD, ROBERT JACQUES VAN. The health of the aged. An investigation into the health and a number of social and psychological factors concerning 3149 aged persons in the Netherlands, carried out by 374 general practitioners under the direction of the Organization for Health Research T.N.O. Assen, Organization for Health Research, 1961. 439p.

Psychological Aging and Personality Changes

AMERICAN PSYCHOLOGICAL ASSOCIATION. DIVISION ON MATURITY AND OLD AGE. Psychological aspects of aging; proceedings of a conference on planning of research, Bethesda, Md., April 24-27, 1955. Washington, 1956. 323p.

BIRREN, JAMES E. The psychology of aging. Englewood Cliffs, N.J., Prentice-Hall, 1964. 303p.

Results of modern research on the complex processes of transportation affecting adults through the second half of their life span.

BORTZ, EDWARD L. Creative aging. New York, Macmillan, 1963. 179p.

Physiology and psychology of aging.

BOTWINICK, JACK. Cognitive processes in maturity and old age. New York, Springer, 1967. 212p.

Discusses problems of cognitive functioning with focus on the later years of life.

BOWERS, MARGARETTA K., *and others.* Counseling the dying. New York, Nelson, 1964. 183p.

A psychoanalyst, a psychiatrist, a clinical psychologist, and a minister set forth their viewpoints.

BRACELAND, FRANCIS J. Psychological aspects of aging. *Nursing Homes,* v. 12, August 1963: 18–23.

Leading psychiatrist discusses various aspects of the aging process in regard to psychological problems involved.

CARP, FRANCES M. The applicability of an empirical scoring standard for a sentence completion test administered to two age groups. *Journal of Gerontology,* v. 22, July 1967: 301–307.

Describes test and concludes that the techniques hold promise for studies investigating differences between persons of different ages.

COPPINGER, NEIL W., ed. The psychological aspects of aging; a prospectus for research in the Veterans Administration. *Gerontologist,* v. 7, June 1967, Pt. II: entire issue.

CUMMING, ELAINE, and WILLIAM E. HENRY. Growing old: the process of disengagement. New York, Basic Books, 1961. 293p.

Theoretical interpretation of the social and psychological nature of the aging process.

DENNIS, WAYNE. Creative productivity between the ages of 20 and 80 years. *Journal of Gerontology,* v. 21, January 1966: 1–8.

Data on the life curve of productivity of 738 persons, all of whom lived to age 70 or beyond.

DOVENMUEHLE, ROBERT H. Physical and psychological aspects of aging. *Lutheran Social Welfare Quarterly,* v. 4, September 1964: 18–27.

The effects of physical changes that occur with againg on psychological outlook and emotional and social behavior.

FORD, CAROLINE S. Ego-adaptive mechanisms of older persons. *Social Casework,* v. 46, January 1965: 16–21.

Demands on the older person in the areas of the social, the physical, and the emotional.

FROMM, ERICH. Psychological problems of aging. *Journal of Rehabilitation,* v. 32, September–October 1966: 10–12; 51–57.

GEIST, HAROLD. The psychological aspects of retirement. Springfield, Ill., Thomas, 1968. 131p.

Outlines psychological and physiological aspects of the aging process; traces history of retirement and pension plans; and discusses problem of the individual who is about to retire or is retired.

HERON, ALASTAIR, and SHEILA CHOWN. Age and function. Boston, Little, 1967. 182p.

Effects of age on personality, perception and performance among representative groups of healthy people and how greatly individuals differ within themselves in the rate at which various functions change with age.

HOCH, PAUL H., and JOSEPH ZUBIN. Psychopathology of aging. New York, Greene, 1961. 321p.
Proceedings of the 50th annual meeting of the American Psychopathological Association, February, 1960. Part I. Epidemiology. Part II. Psychology. Part III. Psychophysiology and genetics. Part IV. Management problems.

KASTENBAUM, ROBERT. The mental life of dying geriatric patients. *Gerontologist*, v. 7, June 1967, pt. I: 97–100.
Few of the psychological aspects of the dying process in aged men and women.

LEHMAN, HARVEY C. Age and achievement. Princeton, Princeton University Press, 1953. 359p.
Statistical evaluation of quality and quantity of achievement in relation to age.

LOETHER, HERMAN J. Problems of aging; sociological and social psychological perspectives. Belmont, Cal., Dickenson, 1967. 118p.

LUDWIG, EDWARD G., and ROBERT L. EICHHORN. Age and disillusionment: a study of value changes associated with aging. *Journal of Gerontology*, v. 22, January 1967: 59–65.

MITCHELL, DOROTHY L., and ALVIN GOLDFARB. Psychological needs of aged patients at home. *American Journal of Public Health*, v. 56, October 1966: 1716–1721.
Report on a pilot study to determine needs of aged patients in their homes, and especially mental and emotional problems.

NEUGARTEN, BERNICE L., *and others*. Personality in middle and late life; empirical studies. New York, Atherton Press, 1964. 231p.
Eight studies of modern psychological approaches to personality and aging.

PECK, ARTHUR. Psychotherapy of the aged. *Journal of the American Geriatrics Society*, v. 14, July 1966: 748–753.
Describes technique specifically designed for the psychotherapy of aged persons.

PRESSEY, SIDNEY L., and ALICE D. PRESSEY. Genius at 80; and other oldsters. *Gerontologist*, v. 7, September 1967, Part I: 183–187.
Study of 10 remarkable men, from Michelangelo to Churchill, who continued their careers into their eighties and of two groups of professional people past 70.

REICHARD, SUZANNE, *and others*. Aging and personality; a study of 87 older men. New York, Wiley, 1962. 237p.
Study concerned with relationship between personality and patterns of aging in a group of manual workers.

43

Schwartz, Arthur N., and Robert W. Kleemeier. The effects of illness and age upon some aspects of personality. *Journal of Gerontology*, v. 20, January 1965: 85–91.

Discusses effects of illness and aging on self-concepts and ego defenses.

Smith, Ethel Sabin. The dynamics of aging. New York, W. W. Norton, 1956. 191p.

Discusses psychological laws which must be observed in order to enjoy the years of retirement.

Symposium on learning and memory. *Gerontologist*, v. 7, March 1967: 3–30.

Age and the immediate memory span, by *George A. Talland*. Verbal learning and retention, by *David Arenberg*. New dimensions and a tentative theory, by *Carl Eisdorfer*. Sociological aspects of learning and memory, by *Sylvia Sherwood*. Job performance and job opportunity: a note, by *Juanita M. Kreps*. Impact on social work, by *Margaret Blenkner*.

Tanenbaum, David E. Loneliness in the aged. *Mental Hygiene*, v. 51, January 1967: 91–99.

Analysis of the experience of loneliness and suggestions for some general needs of aged people.

Thumin, Fred J., and Angela Wittenberg. Personality as related to age and mental ability in female job applicants. *Journal of Gerontology*, v. 20, January 1965: 105–107.

Related specific personality characteristics to chronological and mental ages.

Trembly, Dean, and Johnson O'Connor. Growth and decline of natural and acquired intellectual characteristics, *Journal of Gerontology*, v. 21, January 1966: 9–12.

"Offers a unifying theory of the differential nature of the growth and decline of intellectual factors" based on previous studies and on research findings of a nationwide testing and research organization.

U.S. National Advisory Committee for the White House Conference on Aging. Background paper on research in gerontology: psychological and social sciences. Washington, U.S. Govt. Print. Off., 1960. 74p. (Background paper no. 16)

Welford, A. T., and James E. Birren, eds. Behavior, aging, and the nervous system; biological determinants of speed of behavior and its changes with age. Springfield, Ill., Thomas, 1965. 637p.

Special attention to slowness of behavior associated with advancing age and with certain types of brain damage and psychopathology.

White House Conference on Aging. Research in gerontology: psychological and social sciences. Washington, U.S. Govt. Print. Off., 1961. 72p. (Reports and guidelines series no. 9)

WILLIAMS, RICHARD H., and CLAUDINE G. WIRTHS. Lives through the years; styles of life and successful aging. New York, Atherton Press, 1965. 298p.

Documented account of the process of aging in its psychological and social aspects, built on the results of extensive interviews over a period of 5½ years.

WOLFF, KURT. The biological, sociological, and psychological aspects of aging. Springfield, Ill., Thomas, 1959. 95p.

Reviews current concepts and urges organized study in geriatric psychiatry.

————. Personality type and reaction toward aging and death; a clinical study. *Geriatrics,* v. 21, August 1966: 189–192.

The elderly person's life-long pattern of living influences his approach to old age and death.

WORCHEL, PHILIP, and DONN BYRNE, eds. Personality change. New York, Wiley, 1964. 616p.

Chap. 16. Personality change with age, by *Raymond G. Kuhlen.*

ZINBERG, NORMAN E., and IRVING KAUFMAN, eds. Normal psychology of the aging process. New York, International Universities Press, 1963. 182p.

First annual scientific meeting of the Boston Society for Gerontologic Psychiatry, Inc.

ECONOMIC
ASPECTS
of AGING

Economic Resources in the Later Years

BRADY, DOROTHY S. Age and the income distribution. Washington, U.S. Govt. Print. Off., 1965. 62p. (Research report no. 8)
Analyzes distribution of individual incomes of men and women in different age groups in 1941 and in each year since 1947.

BROTMAN, HERMAN B. Counting the aged poor. *Aging,* no. 150, April 1967: 10–12.

BURGESS, ERNEST WATSON, ed. Aging in Western societies. Chicago, University of Chicago Press, 1960. 492p.
Survey of the socioeconomic roots of the problems of older persons, and of the solution adopted by societies with Western culture.

CHAMBER OF COMMERCE OF THE UNITED STATES. TASK FORCE ON ECONOMIC GROWTH AND OPPORTUNITY. Poverty: the sick, disabled and aged. Washington, 1965. 263p. (2nd rept.)
The aged poor, p. 64–87. "The aged poor," study paper by *Juanita M. Kreps,* p. 239–263.

CHEN, YUNG-PING. Economic poverty: the special case of the aged. *Gerontologist,* v. 6, March 1966: 39–45.

———. Low income, early retirement, and tax policy. *Gerontologist,* v. 6, March 1966: 35–38.
Concerned with the policy of offering concessions to the aged as well as with the tax instruments implementing the policy.

———. Preferential treatment of the aged in income and property taxation. *American Journal of Economics and Sociology,* v. 25, January 1966: 27–38.
Factual information about preferential tax provisions, with a series of critical analyses of them.

CLARK, HAROLD A. Retirement income goals. *Journal of the American Society of Chartered Life Underwriters,* v. 19, Fall 1965: 307–318.
Considers planned increases in social security benefits and present private retirement plans' benefit levels, income goods, and trends.

COHEN, WILBUR J. Improving the status of the aged. *Social Security Bulletin,* v. 29, December 1966: 3–8.
Recent progress, present situation, and blueprint for action.

COLLINS, BEULAH. The senior forum: questions and answers about retirement. New York, Fleet, 1964. 316p.

Large portion devoted to the subject of money.

CONFERENCE ON POVERTY IN AMERICA. Poverty in America; proceedings . . . San Francisco, Chandler, 1965. 465p.

Poverty and income maintenance for the aged, by *Charles I. Schottland*, p. 227–239.

CORSON, JOHN J., and JOHN W. MCCONNELL. Economic needs of older people. New York, Twentieth Century Fund, 1956. 533p.

Surveys income and employment status of the aged, including social insurance and retirement plans. Contains the report and recommendations of the Committee on Economic Needs of Older People chosen by the Twentieth Century Fund to review the facts and formulate a program for action.

ECKSTEIN, OTTO, ed. Studies in the economics of income maintenance. Washington, Brookings, 1967. 254p.

Benefits under the American social security system, by *Henry Aaron.* Public assistance expenditures in the United States, by *Lora S. Collins.*

EPSTEIN, ABRAHAM. The challenge of the aged. New York, Macy-Masius, Vanguard, 1928. 435p.

History of old age dependency in the United States; State legislation for the aged; foreign experience.

EPSTEIN, LENORE A. Income security standards in old age. Washington, U.S. Social Security Administration, Division of Research and Statistics, 1963. 26p. (Research report no. 3)

National standard for income security in retirement as it relates to the size of the benefit.

———. and JANET H. MURRAY. The aged population of the United States; the 1963 social security survey of the aged. Washington, U.S. Govt. Print. Off., 1967. 423p. (Research report no. 19)

Size and sources of incomes and assets, living arrangements, medical expenditures, and other major aspects of the lives of persons aged 62 and over.

GALLAWAY, LOWELL E. The aged and the extent of poverty in the United States, *Southern Economic Journal,* v. 33, October 1966: 212–222.

Concerned with families in which the head is aged 65 or over and the reasons why their incomes have not moved in unison with economy-wide income levels.

GOLDSTEIN, SIDNEY. Changing income and consumption patterns of the aged, 1950–1960. *Journal of Gerontology,* v. 20, October 1965: 453–461.

Preliminary findings of the BLS survey of consumer expenditures compared with patterns of the 1950 survey.

GOLDSTEIN, SIDNEY. Urban and rural differentials in consumer patterns of the aged, 1960–61. *Rural Sociology*, v. 31, September 1966: 333–345.

BLS survey of consumer expenditures in 1960–61 analyzed to determine the effect of residence on the income, expenditure, and savings of older units.

GRANT, MARGARET. Old-age security; social and financial trends. A report prepared for the Committee on Social Security. Washington, Committee on Social Security, Social Science Research Council, 1939. 261p.

Study of foreign social insurance systems in relation to the problems presented in the U.S.

GREENFIELD, MARGARET. Property tax exemptions for senior citizens. Berkeley, Cal., Institute of Governmental Studies, University of California, 1966. 91p.

In a survey in two tracts in Oakland where there was a high correlation between home ownership and elderly persons those replying to questionnaires considered day-to-day living costs and recurring property taxes more of a problem than expenditures for medical care.

GUTHRIE, HAROLD W. The retired population-boon for local economies? *Quarterly Review of Economics and Business*, v. 4, Spring 1964: 51–56.

Study based on 1960 pilot survey on the financial status of retired families, done by the Survey Research Center of the University of Michigan.

HURFF, GEORGE B., ed. Economic problems of retirement. Gainesville, University of Florida Press, 1954. 180p. (Institute of Gerontology series no. 4)

Report on the fourth annual Southern Conference on Gerontology held at the University of Florida, January 27–28, 1954.

KATONA, GEORGE. Private pensions and individual saving. Ann Arbor, Mich., Survey Research Center, Institute for Social Research, University of Michigan, 1965. 114p. (Monograph no. 40)

Study of the economic behavior of those participating in pension plans prior to their retirement.

KREPS, JUANITA M., ed. Employment, income, and retirement problems of the aged. Durham, N.C., Duke University Press, 1963. 240p.

Recent trends in income, employment, labor force size and their relation to the changing age structure of the population.

LEVITAN, SAR A. An evaluation of the social security system as an income protection program. *Pension and Welfare News*, v. 2, September 1966: 44–47.

Discusses adequacy of present programs for the aged poor.

LINDEN, FABIAN. Spending power in the seventies. *Conference Board Record,* v. 3, March 1966: 46–48; April 1966: 37–40.
Changing patterns of age and income, 1965–1975.

LOMBERG, DORIS E., and JANET A. KROFTA. Farm family finances in the middle years. *Journal of Home Economics,* v. 57, February 1965: 123–128.
Wisconsin studies of farm families in the middle years show conflicting personal goals.

McCAMMAN, DOROTHY. The economics of aging. *Lutheran Social Welfare Quarterly,* v. 4, September 1964: 3–10.
Various factors underlying the financial position in which the elderly find themselves.

MILLER, HERMAN P. Income distribution in the United States. Washington, U.S. Govt. Print. Off., 1966. 306p.
An analysis of changes in the distribution of income in the U.S. based largely on information collected in the last three decennial censuses.

MORGAN, JAMES N. Measuring the economic status of the aged. *International Economic Review,* v. 6, January 1965: 1–17.
Report on work at the Survey Research Center of the University of Michigan in developing new measures of economic status and what differences the improvements made in the data for the U.S.

NATIONAL COUNCIL ON THE AGING. Resources for the aging; an action handbook: federal programs, foundations and trusts, and voluntary agencies that assist the aging. New York, 1967. 276p.

NIZAN, ARYEH. Living conditions of the aged in Israel. Jerusalem, National Insurance Institute, 1963. Various paging.
Study concerned with about 50,000 recipients of old age insurance pensions paid through the National Insurance Institute, and about 8,000 recipients of old age assistance pensions paid by the Ministry of Social Welfare. Tables are in Hebrew.

ORBACH, HAROLD L., and CLARK TIBBITTS, eds. Aging and the economy. Ann Arbor, University of Michigan Press, 1963. 237p.
Papers and addresses prepared for the University of Michigan's 15th annual conference on aging held in Ann Arbor, June 18–20, 1962.

ORSHANSKY, MOLLIE. The aged Negro and his income. *Social Security Bulletin,* v. 27, February 1964: 3–13.
Income of aged nonwhite population, the role of OASDI and old-age assistance.

OSTERBIND, CARTER C., ed. Income in retirement; the need and society's responsibility. Gainesville, University of Florida Press, 1967. 132p. (Institute of Gerontology series *vol.* 16)

Report on the 16th annual Southern Conference on Gerontology held at the University of Florida, February 12–14, 1967.

PARKER, FLORENCE EVELYN. Care of aged persons in the United States. Washington, U.S. Govt. Print. Off., 1929. 305p. (*Bulletin of the U.S. Bureau of Labor Statistics*, no. 489)

Deals with public old-age pensions and homes for the aged.

REINSEL, EDWARD I., and JOHN C. ELLICKSON. Farmers and social security. *Agricultural Finance Review*, v. 26, September 1965: 32–41; *Social Security Bulletin*, v. 29, March 1966: 11–14.

Age and income characteristics of self-employed farm operators with net earnings of at least $400 a year.

SCHNEIDER, MARGARET GRANT. More security for old age; a report and a program. New York, Twentieth Century Fund, 1937. 191p.

Summary of foreign old age insurance and pension plans and of American experience with old age security is combined with a program for action.

SCHULZ, JAMES H. Some economics of aged home ownership. *Gerontologist*, v. 7, March 1967: 73–74; 80.

Data on economic aspects of home ownership by aged persons for two age groups, 65–74 and 75 or over.

SELIGMAN, BEN B., ed. Poverty as a public issue. New York, Free Press, 1965. 359p.

The poverty of aging, by *Harold L. Sheppard.*

STEINER, PETER O., and ROBERT DORFMAN. The economic status of the aged. Berkeley, University of California Press, 1957. 296p.

Income, living arrangements, and labor force status of older persons.

Survey of consumer finances. Ann Arbor, Mich., Survey Research Center, Institute for Social Research, University of Michigan.

Issued annually.

TRAFTON, MARIE C. Old-age, survivors, and disability insurance: earnings of older workers and retired-worker beneficiaries. *Social Security Bulletin*, v. 28, May 1965: 9–17; 33.

Analyses of the earnings of older persons.

TURNBULL, JOHN G., *and others.* The changing faces of economic insecurity. Minneapolis, University of Minnesota Press, 1966. 157p.

Analyzes the quantitative and qualitative ways in which changes are occurring in premature death, old age, unemployment, and accidental injury and sickness.

U.S. BUREAU OF LABOR STATISTICS. Care of aged persons in the United States. Washington, U.S. Govt. Print. Off., 1929. 305p. *(Bureau of Labor Statistics Bulletin* no. 489)

> Includes care of the aged in homes for the aged, by the federal government, by state governments, by labor organizations, by religious and fraternal organizations, by nationality groups, and discusses retirement systems and pension plans.

U.S. BUREAU OF THE CENSUS. Income of the elderly in 1963. Washington, D.C., U.S. Govt. Print. Off., 1965. 21p. (Series P–60, no. 46)

————. Present value of estimated lifetime earnings. Washington, U.S. Govt. Print. Off., 1967. 54p. (Technical paper no. 16)

> Expected lifetime earnings for males 18 to 64 years old in the experienced civilian labor force with earnings in 1959.

————. Trends in the income of families and persons in the United States, 1947–1964. Washington, U.S. Govt. Print. Off., 1967. 294p. (Technical paper no. 17)

> Distribution of families and unrelated individuals by income levels cross-classified by various characteristics such as farm-nonfarm residence, age, sex, color, employment status, occupation and industry of head, size of family, number of related children, number of earners, etc.

U.S. COMMITTEE ON ECONOMIC SECURITY. Report to the President. Washington, U.S. Govt. Print. Off., 1935. 74p.

————. Social security in America; the factual background of the Social Security Act as summarized from staff reports to the Committee on Economic Security. Washington, U.S. Govt. Print. Off., 1937. 592p. (U.S. Social Security Board, publication no. 20)

U.S. CONGRESS. JOINT ECONOMIC COMMITTEE. Old age income assurance: a compendium of papers on problems and policy issues in the public and private pension system. Washington, U.S. Govt. Print. Off., 1967. 5 v. (90th Cong., 1st sess., joint committee print)

————. ————. Old age income assurance: an outline of issues and alternatives. Washington, U.S. Govt. Print. Off., 1966. 39p. (89th Cong., 2d sess., joint committee print)

> Outline drawn from the literature concerning existing and possible future programs for old-age income assurance.

————. SENATE. SPECIAL COMMITTEE ON AGING. Frauds and deceptions affecting the elderly; investigations, findings, recommendations, 1964. Washington, U.S. Govt. Print. Off., 1965. 90p. (89th Cong., 1st sess., committee print)

> A report of the Subcommittee on Frauds and Misrepresentations Affecting the Elderly.

U.S. Congress. Senate. Special Committee on Aging. Tax consequences of contributions to needy older relatives. Washington, U.S. Govt. Print. Off., 1966. 21p. (89th Cong., 2d sess., S. Rept. no. 1721)

Interested in determining whether federal tax laws are fair to families within which contributions to older relatives are made.

———. ———. ———. The war on poverty as it affects older Americans. Washington, U.S. Govt. Print. Off., 1966. 146p. (89th Cong., 2nd sess., report no. 1287)

Appendix A—Older persons program (report of Office of Economic Opportunity). Appendix B—Poverty and the older American (first report of the Office of Economic Opportunity Task Force on Programs for Older Persons, August 1965).

U.S. National Advisory Committee for the White House Conference on Aging. Background paper on income maintenance. Washington, U.S. Govt. Print. Off., 1960. 110p. (Background paper no. 2)

———. Background paper on impact of inflation on retired persons. Washington, U.S. Govt. Print. Off., 1960. 56p. (Background paper no. 3)

U.S. President's Council on Aging. Federal payments to older persons in need of protection; a report of a survey and conference. Washington, U.S. Govt. Print. Off., 1965. 66p.

Survey of federal agencies administering major benefit-paying programs; conference discussion of the survey report and its implications; summary of conclusions and recommendations from the survey and the conference.

U.S. Social Security Administration. Social security programs in the United States. Washington, U.S. Govt. Print. Off., 1966. 120p.

Primary emphasis on the income maintenance aspects of social security programs, with some attention to health insurance and medical assistance programs.

Vatter, Ethel L. Private pension accruals; a device for increasing financial security in old age. *Journal of Home Economics,* v. 59, January 1967: 20–23.

Reviews types of private pension plans and recommends improving private coverage as a means of reducing the number of aged in poverty.

White House Conference on Aging. Impact of inflation on retired persons. A statement of problems, issues and approaches together with recommendations from the White House Conference on Aging. Washington, U.S. Govt. Print. Off., 1961. 39p. (Reports and guidelines, series no. 4)

WHITE HOUSE CONFERENCE ON AGING. Income maintenance, including financing of health costs. A statement of problems, issues and approaches together with recommendations from the 1961 White House Conference on Aging. Washington, U.S. Govt. Print. Off., 1961. 98p. (Reports and guidelines, series no. 5)

Employment and Retirement Practices

BEARD, FANNIE B. A vocational training and placement program for older workers. Washington, U.S. Govt. Print. Off., 1961. 10p. (Patterns for progress in aging, case study no. 2)
> Represents an example of coordination of official and voluntary agencies in Arkansas.

BELBIN, R. M. Training methods for older workers. Paris, Organisation for Economic Co-operation and Development, 1965. 72p.
> Source book of information on the training of older adults.

BRECKINRIDGE, ELIZABETH LLEWELLYN. Effective use of older workers. New York, Wilcox and Follett, 1953. 224p.
> Study based on a National survey sponsored by the University of Chicago's Committee on Human Development.

BRENNAN, MICHAEL J., and others. The economics of age. New York, Norton, 1967. 246p.
> Study of economic forces determining income and employment at different age levels, with focus on barriers confronting the older worker.

BUSSE, EWALD W., and JUANITA M. KREPS. Criteria for retirement: a re-examination. *Gerontologist,* v. 4, September 1964: 115–120.
> Discussion of new criteria based on the economic developments of the past decade.

CLARK, FREDERICK LEGROS. Growing old in a mechanized world; the human problem of a technical revolution. London, Nuffield Foundation, 1960. 145p.
> Conveys comprehensive picture of the varied working conditions under which the older workers of today have to hold down or resign their places in the labor force.

————. Woman, work and age. Nuffield Foundation, 1962. 111p.
> Study of work force participation of middle-aged women in the United Kingdom: reasons for working, nature of work, withdrawal from work.

————. Work, age and leisure. London, Michael Joseph, 1966. 152p.
> Causes and consequences of the shortened working life.

CLARK, FREDERICK LEGROS, and AGNES C. DUNNE. Aging in industry; an inquiry, based on figures derived from census reports, into the problem of aging under conditions of modern industry. New York, Philosophical Library, 1956. 146p.

Purpose is to determine what number of workers are physically able to continue in their occupations beyond their mid-sixties. Based on Great Britain's census reports for 1921, 1931, and 1951.

CROOK, GUY HAMILTON, and MARTIN HEINSTEIN. The older worker in industry; a study of the attitudes of industrial workers toward aging and retirement. Berkeley, Institute of Industrial Relations, University of California, 1958. 143p.

DAVIDSON, WAYNE R., and KARL R. KUNZE. Psychological, social, and economic meanings of work in modern society: their effects on the worker facing retirement. *Gerontologist,* v. 5, September 1965: Pt. I: 129–133; 159.

Focus on attitudes and motivation relating to work and retirement and on a retirement counseling program.

DONAHUE, WILMA T., ed. Earning opportunities for older workers. Ann Arbor, University of Michigan Press, 1955. 277p.

Discusses methods of adapting jobs to fit abilities of aging workers and for creating earning opportunities for older people. Based largely on papers presented at the University of Michigan's sixth annual conference on aging.

DRAPER, JEAN E., *and others.* Work attitudes and retirement adjustments. Madison, Wis., University of Wisconsin, Graduate School of Business, Bureau of Business Research and Service, 1967. 91p. (Wisconsin Commerce Reports, v. 8, no. 1)

Survey of attitudes toward work, attitudes toward retirement, adjustment to retirement, and the interrelationships among these.

EPSTEIN, LENORE A. Early retirement and work-life experience. *Social Security Bulletin,* v. 29, March 1966: 3–10.

Analysis of the employment history of workers entitled to retirement benefits in 1962 and 1963.

FALTERMAYER, EDMUND K. The drift to early retirement. *Fortune,* v. 71, May 1965: 112–115; 218; 222.

Policies of companies and unions, and how employers feel.

FRIEDMANN, EUGENE, *and others.* The meaning of work and retirement. Chicago, University of Chicago Press, 1954. 197p.

Significance of work in the lives of people in several different occupations and the relationship between the significance of work and attitudes toward retirement.

GOLDSTEIN, SIDNEY. Socio-economic and migration differentials between the aged in the labor force and in the labor reserve. *Gerontologist,* v. 7, March 1967: 31–40; 79.

Age and sex differentials in the labor reserve; occupational and educational differentials between aged members of the labor force and labor reserve; differential patterns of migration among members of the labor force, labor reserve, and those who withdrew from the labor force more than 10 years prior to the 1960 census.

GRIEW, STEPHEN. Job re-design; the application of biological data on aging to the design of equipment and the organisation of work. Paris, Organisation for Economic Co-operation and Development, 1964. 86p.

HANSEN, PERCY M. Never too late to be young. New York, Fell, 1966. 215p.

Opposes the system of forced retirement and the taxing of the younger generation for the benefit of the elderly.

INTERNATIONAL MANAGEMENT SEMINAR ON JOB REDESIGN AND OCCUPATIONAL TRAINING FOR OLDER WORKERS. Final report. Paris, Organisation for Economic Co-operation and Development, 1965. 95p. (International seminars 1964–2)

Discussion of the practical experience of employers.

JEWISH VOCATIONAL SERVICE. The therapeutic workshop for older persons. Chicago, 1966. 74p. (Monograph no. 5)

Results of a 5-year project to increase the work capacities of older persons.

JOINT CONFERENCE ON THE PROBLEM OF MAKING A LIVING WHILE GROWING OLD. Proceedings. Philadelphia, Temple University and Pennsylvania Department of Labor and Industry.

First conference held in 1952.

JURGENSEN, CLIFFORD E. Personnel tests and the older worker. *Employment Service Review,* v. 4, November-December 1967: 18–19; 30.

Research findings on the accuracy of personnel tests for the older worker.

KREPS, JUANITA M., ed. Technology, manpower, and retirement policy. Cleveland, World, 1966. 197p.

Problems of older workers arising from policies which industry, labor unions, and the government have adopted to reduce labor-force size.

LATIMER, MURRAY W. The relationship of employee hiring ages to the cost of pension plans. Washington, U.S. Bureau of Labor Statistics, 1965. 209p.

Does not assume that the cost of a pension plan is to be equated to the deposits of money in a pension fund.

LEVINE, LOUIS. Opening jobs to older disabled workers. *Employment Service Review,* v. 1, April 1964: 1–6.

————. Revitalizing older worker services. *Employment Service Review,* v. 2, October 1965: 1–4; 18.

Describes actions of the federal government and the role of the U.S. Employment Service in the employment of older persons.

LEWIS, ADELE, and EDITH BOBROFF. From kitchen to career. Indianapolis, Bobbs, 1965. 204p.

Advice on how older women should hunt for the right job.

LOBSENZ, JOHANNA. The older woman in industry. New York, Scribner's, 1929. 281p.

Does not include the professions but does include clerical, general office work, selling and domestic work.

MATHIASEN, GENEVA, ed. Criteria for retirement. A report of a national conference on retirement of older workers. New York, Putnam, 1953. 233p.

Premise of the conference was that chronological age has not proved acceptable as a sole basis for retirement policy.

————. Flexible retirement; evolving policies and programs for industry and labor. New York, Putnam, 1959. 226p.

MELTZER, H. Attitudes of workers before and after age 40. *Geriatrics,* v. 20, May 1965: 425–432.

Work attitudes and life adjustments of employees under 40 differ to a statistically significant degree from those of workers over that age, to the advantage of the elders.

MURRAY, MERRILL G. Should pensioners receive unemployment compensation? Kalamazoo, Mich., W. E. Upjohn Institute for Employment Research, 1967. 42p.

Points up wide divergence in policy among states, and analyzes relevant facts, considerations, and methods involved.

MUTHARD, JOHN E., and WOODROW W. MORRIS, eds. Counseling the older disabled worker. Iowa City, Iowa, State University of Iowa, 1961. 131p.

Report, developed from major speeches at two 1-week conferences, emphasizes: medical and psychiatric evaluation of older workers; counseling techniques; utilization of community services and resources; and employment problems and placement procedures.

NATIONAL CONFERENCE ON MANPOWER TRAINING AND THE OLDER WORKER. Proceedings . . . New York, National Council on the Aging, 1966. 756p.

Sponsored by Committee on Employment and Retirement of the National Council on the Aging in cooperation with the U.S. Dept. of Health, Education, and Welfare, under a project financed through the Office of Manpower Planning, Evaluation and Research of the U.S. Dept. of Labor.

NATIONAL MANPOWER COUNCIL. Manpower policies for a democratic society; the final statement of the council. New York, Columbia University Press, 1965. 121p.

The older worker. *Employment Service Review,* v. 4, May 1967: 18-23; 48.

> Houston, primer for counselors of older workers, by *Anna J. Metherd.* Rochester, N.Y.; placing the mature worker in a high employment area, by *Grace Kime.*

ROSENBLATT, AARON. The functions of work and employment for older persons. *Journal of Jewish Communal Service,* v. 42, Spring 1966: 259-268.

> Survey designed to provide information on the employment needs and interest in, and attitudes toward, employment of 250 older persons, aged 60–74.

SHEPPARD, HAROLD L., *and others.* Too old to work—too young to retire: a case study of a permanent plant shutdown. (Prepared for the U.S. Senate Special Committee on Unemployment Problems) Washington, U.S. Govt. Print. Off., 1960. 74p. (86th Cong., 1st sess., committee print)

SOBEL, IRVIN, and RICHARD C. WILCOCK. Placement techniques for older workers. Paris, Organisation of Economic Cooperation and Development, 1964. 81p.

> How employment services may improve their placement methods and their use of other facilities and agencies.

———. ———. Job placement services for older workers in the United States. *International Labour Review,* v. 88, August 1963: 129-156.

> First findings of a sampling of 40 public employment offices in 12 communities in 6 different states.

SVOLOS, SEBASTIA. Employment of older workers and size of employing unit. *Social Security Bulletin,* v. 28, September 1965: 25-29; 37-38.

U.S. ADMINISTRATION ON AGING. Are you planning on living the rest of your life? Washington, U.S. Govt. Print. Off., 1965. 72p. (AoA no. 803)

> A preretirement planning booklet to be used at home with wife, husband, or friend. Prepared in cooperation with the Chicago Commission for Senior Citizens.

———. You, the law, and retirement. Washington, U.S. Govt. Print. Off., 1965. 36p. (AoA no. 800)

> Why, how, and when to see a lawyer in making decisions when getting ready to retire and after retirement.

U.S. BUREAU OF LABOR STATISTICS. Job redesign for older workers; ten case studies. Washington, U.S. Govt. Print. Off., 1967. 63p. (Bulletin no. 1523)

> Experience of companies who have been successful in redesigning jobs for older workers.

U.S. BUREAU OF THE CENSUS. U.S. Census of population: 1960. Subject reports. Labor reserve; age, education, occupation, and other characteristics of former members of the labor force. Washington, U.S. Govt. Print. Off., 1966. 199p. (Final report PC [2]-6C)

U.S. CONGRESS. SENATE. SPECIAL COMMITTEE ON AGING. Increasing employment opportunities for the elderly—recommendations and comment. Washington, U.S. Govt. Print. Off., 1964. 5p. (88th Cong., 2d sess., committee print)

————. ————. ————. Reduction of retirement benefits due to social security increases. Washington, U.S. Govt. Print. Off., 1967. 23p. (90th Cong., 1st sess., committee print)
Report by the Subcommittee on Employment and Retirement Incomes.

U.S. DEPT. OF LABOR. The older American worker; age discrimination in employment. Report of the Secretary of Labor to the Congress under Section 715 of the Civil Rights Act of 1964. Washington, 1965. 25p.

————. The older American worker; age discrimination in employment. Report of the Secretary of Labor to the Congress under Section 715 of the Civil Rights Act of 1964; research materials. Washington, 1965. 153p.
Special studies and inquiries undertaken for the report.

————. OFFICE OF MANPOWER, AUTOMATION AND TRAINING. Mobility and worker adaptation to economic change in the United States. Washington, 1963. 77p. (Manpower Research Bulletin, no. 1, rev. July 1963)
Background information on unemployment problems in a changing manpower situation, with a view to pointing out areas where government can assist in finding new jobs for the unemployed and help them adapt to changing job requirements.

————. OFFICE OF MANPOWER POLICY, EVALUATION, AND RESEARCH. Unused manpower: the nation's loss. Washington, 1966. 25p. (Manpower Research Bulletin, no. 10)
Trend of male nonparticipation in the labor force, important differences in these rates by color and age, and some of the reasons why these disparities may exist.

WELFORD, ALAN TRAVISS. Ageing and human skill; a report centered on work by the Nuffield Unit for Research into Problems of Ageing. London, Oxford University Press, 1958. 300p.
Studies changes of performance from young adulthood through the middle years to the 60's and 70's.

————. Industrial work suitable for older people: some British studies. *Gerontologist*, v. 6, March 1966: 4–9.
Describes research studies, their achievements and significance for industry.

WENTWORTH, EDNA C. Employment after retirement; a study of the postentitlement work experience of men drawing benefits under social security. Washington, U.S. Govt. Print. Off., 1968. 48p. (Research Report no. 21)

WERMEL, MICHAEL T., and GERALDINE M. BEIDEMAN, eds. Industry's interest in the older worker and the retired employee; proceedings of a conference. Pasadena, Calif., Institute of Technology, Benefits and Insurance Research Center, 1960. 35p. (BIRC publication no. 13)

WHITE HOUSE CONFERENCE ON AGING. Employment security and retirement of the older worker; a report of the proceedings and outcomes of the White House Conference on Aging, as related to the status, needs and prospects of the aging American worker. Washington, U.S. Govt. Print. Off., 1961. 55p. (Reports and guidelines, series no. 3)

WHITMAN, HOWARD. Helping older people find jobs. Burlingame, Calif., Foundation for Voluntary Welfare, 1962. 68p.

> Manual for starting a community employment service for older men and women.

WILSON, PAUL A. A vocational counseling program for older workers. Washington, U.S. Govt. Print. Off., 1961. 22p. (Patterns for Progress in Aging, case study no. 7)

> Study of Cleveland's program of vocational counseling for middle-age and older workers.

WOLFF, HAROLD. Utilization of older professional and scientific workers. New York, National Council on the Aging, 1961. 20p.

> Factual information on the dimensions of the potential and the problems associated with the older scientific and professional worker.

Health Insurance

AHMED, PAUL I. Patterns of health insurance coverage for American families. *Inquiry,* v. 4, December 1967: 59–68.

> Discusses methodology of health insurance data on a family basis and presents the results obtained.

ALEXANDER, C. A. The effects of change in method of paying physicians: the Baltimore experience. *American Journal of Public Health,* v. 57, August 1967: 1278–1289.

> Analysis of the observed effects in Baltimore's Medical Care Program for the Indigent, following a change from capitation to fee-for-service.

ALLEN, DAVID. Health insurance for the aged: participating extended care facilities. *Social Security Bulletin,* v. 30, June 1967: 3–8.

Describes the benefits and presents data on the number of extended-care facilities certified for participation under the program and on the characteristics of such facilities.

AMERICAN MEDICAL ASSOCIATION. COMMISSION ON THE COSTS OF MEDICAL CARE. Report. Chicago, 1963–64. 4 v.

V. 1. General report. V. 2. Professional review mechanisms. V. 3. Significant medical advances. V. 4. Changing patterns of medical care.

ANDERSEN, RONALD, and DONALD C. RIEDEL. People and their hospital insurance; comparisons of the uninsured, those with one policy, and those with multiple coverage. Chicago, Center for Health Administration Studies, University of Chicago, 1967. 37p. (Research series no. 23)

———, and ODIN W. ANDERSON. A decade of health services; social survey trends in use and expenditure. Chicago, University of Chicago Press, 1967. 244p.

How people in the United States use the health services system.

ANDERSON, ODIN W., *and others.* Changes in family medical care expenditures and voluntary health insurance; a five-year re-survey. Cambridge, Harvard University Press, 1963. 217p.

Details changes in the medical economy from 1953 to 1958, and highlights 1958 data in terms of contemporary problems, and efforts being made to resolve these problems.

AVNET, HELEN H., and MATA K. NIKIAS. Insured dental care: a research project report. New York, Group Health Dental Insurance, 1967. 371p.

Statistical study based on experience recorded in the claims records of GHDI.

BAEHR, GEORGE. Medical care: old goals and new horizons. *American Journal of Public Health,* v. 55, December 1965: 1861–1873.

The recommendations of the Committee on the Costs of Medical Care in 1932, the reasons for limited progress since then, and the means to achieve them in the future.

———. Prepaid group practice: its strength and weaknesses, and its future. *American Journal of Public Health,* v. 56, November 1966: 1898–1903.

Reviews evolution of group practice in terms of achievements and defects.

BALL, ROBERT M. Health insurance for the aged in the United States of America. *Bulletin of the International Social Security Association,* v. 19, September-October 1966: 327–338.

Brief legislative history of the health insurance law.

BLUE CROSS ASSOCIATION. Blue Cross and Medicare; a report to the nation. Chicago, 1966. 32p.

Describes provisions of the contract between Blue Cross and the U.S. Government to operate a nationwide administrative service for Medicare.

BURNS, EVELINE M. The role of government in health services. *Bulletin of the New York Academy of Medicine,* v. 41, July 1965: 753–794.

Discusses government's role in relation to medical care, insurance, institutions, and physicians.

CARLOVA, JOHN, *and others.* Medicare in action. *Medical Economics,* v. 42, August 23, 1965. 75–109.

Predictions as to the effects of Medicare on doctors, patients, hospitals, and health plans based on answers to questionnaires by physicians and hospital administrators.

COHEN, WILBUR J. The first 100 days of Medicare. *Public Health Reports,* v. 81, December 1966: 1051–1056.

Discusses principles and methods, and future needs.

COMMERCE CLEARING HOUSE. Complete guide to Medicare; law, regulations, explanation. New York, 1967. 323p.

Includes supplement (8p. 1st group). Includes legislation.

THE COMMITTEE ON THE COSTS OF MEDICAL CARE. Publications. Chicago, University of Chicago Press, 1928–1933.

Twenty-eight separate studies on all aspects of medical care.

DICKERSON, O. D. Changing concepts of health care financing. *Journal of the American Society of Chartered Life Underwriters,* v. 19, Spring 1965: 170–177.

Points out some of the different concepts in health insurance and their different evolution and change.

EILERS, ROBERT D. Dental service corporations: their place and problems. *Journal of the American Society of Chartered Life Underwriters,* v. 18, June 1964: 262–280.

Discusses dental service plans now in operation.

FALK, I. S., and ANITA PEPPER. Health insurance through collective bargaining in an urban area. *American Journal of Public Health,* v. 56, December 1966: 2006–2022.

Survey of collective bargaining plans of labor unions in New Haven and eleven surrounding areas.

FEINGOLD, EUGENE. Medicare: policy and politics; a case study and policy analysis. San Francisco, Chandler, 1966. 317p.

Economics of medical care and the history of the legislation resulting in the enactment into law of health insurance for the aged.

64

FOLLMANN, J. F., JR. Health insurance and vision care. *Pension and Welfare News,* v. 3, January 1967: 51–54.

Discusses various approaches to prepayment or insurance benefits for the costs of vision care.

————. Medical care and health insurance; a study in social progress. Homewood, Ill., Irwin, 1963. 518p.

Analysis of government programs for medical care in 33 countries, with comparisons with U.S. approaches, particularly private health insurance.

————. Prescription drug insurance. *Pension and Welfare News,* v. 4, November 1967: 43–45; 62.

Discusses prescription costs, insurance coverages, and future needs.

————. Private health insurance, 1967. New York, Health Insurance Association of America, 1967.

Background paper for the National Conference on Private Health Insurance.

Government and medicine in the United States. *Current History,* v. 45, August 1963: entire issue.

Articles by *Odin W. Anderson, William G. Carleton, Roy Lubove, Marion B. Folsom, Wilbur J. Cohen, Edward R. Annis, Seymour E. Harris.*

GREENFIELD, MARGARET. Health insurance for the aged: the 1965 program for Medicare. Berkeley, Institute of Governmental Studies, University of California, 1966. 122p.

Chap. 1. The 1965 Social Security Amendments. Chap. 2. Medical insurance for the aged. Chap. 3. Reasons for a federal program. Chap. 4. The struggle for enactment.

GREGG, DAVIS W., ed. Life and health insurance handbook. 2d ed. Homewood, Ill., Irwin, 1964. 1348p.

Principles of all major phases of life and health insurance, including pension and profitsharing.

HANFT, RUTH S. National health expenditures, 1950–1965. *Social Security Bulletin,* v. 30, February 1967: 3–13.

Trends in the amount and distribution of health expenditures.

HARRIS, RICHARD. A sacred trust. New York, New American Library, 1966. 218p.

Story of the fight of the American Medical Association against health insurance legislation.

HEALTH INSURANCE INSTITUTE. Health insurance and health care statistics by state for the nation's 50 states and the District of Columbia. New York, 1968. 55p.

Coverage, by state, by type of policy, benefits, and data.

HEALTH INSURANCE INSTITUTE. Source book of health insurance data. New York.

   Annual review of the latest available information on the major forms of private health insurance.

HESS, ARTHUR E. Medicare's early months: a program round-up. *Social Security Bulletin,* v. 30, July 1967: 4–8.

   Brief description of operations and future outlook.

JOHNSON, HARRY M. Major medical expense insurance. *Journal of Risk and Insurance,* v. 32, June 1965: 211–236.

   Describes the development of major medical expense insurance and its coverage.

KOPLIN, ALLEN N. Retainer payment for physicians' services. *American Journal of Public Health,* v. 57, August 1967: 1363–1373.

   Deals with flexible fee-for-time method of paying physicians and its use by the UMA Welfare and Retirement Fund for more than 15 years.

MACCOLL, WILLIAM A. Group practice and prepayment of medical care. Washington, Public Affairs Press, 1966. 257p.

   History of consumer-oriented prepaid group-practice plans.

Medicare Symposium. *Geriatrics,* v. 21, July 1966: 144–165.

   Five articles on the future of medicare by *John M. Cashman, Wilbur J. Cohen, John E. Fogarty, George James, Frederick C. Swartz.*

MUNTS, RAYMOND. Bargaining for health; labor unions, health insurance and medical care. Madison, University of Wisconsin Press, 1967. 320p.

   The evolution of health bargaining.

MYERS, ROBERT J., and CHARLES B. BAUGHMAN. History of cost estimates for hospital insurance. Washington, U.S. Social Security Administration, Office of the Actuary, 1966. 54p. (Actuarial study no. 61)

   History of the development of the cost estimates made by the Office of the Actuary for various proposals for providing hospital insurance benefits to persons aged 65 and over.

NATIONAL CONFERENCE ON MEDICAL COSTS. Chart book. Washington, U.S. Dept. of Health, Education, and Welfare, 1967. n.p.

———. Report. Washington, U.S. Dept. of Health, Education, and Welfare, 1968. 326p.

   Conference papers.

NATIONAL CONFERENCE ON PRIVATE HEALTH INSURANCE AND MEDICAL CARE. Conference papers. Washington, U.S. Govt. Print. Off., 1968. 96p.
Review of the current organization of health services and their financing.

NATIONAL COUNCIL ON THE AGING. Principles and criteria for determining medical indigency. *American Journal of Public Health,* v. 54, October 1964: 1745–1765.
Report of a project committee on how to determine an individual's need for financial assistance with medical care.

Panel discussion—Medicare. *Journal of the American Geriatrics Society,* v. 15, November 1967: 971–994.
Panelists discuss present status of Medicare: from the standpoint of the physician; from the standpoint of the carrier; and the impact on outpatient departments.

REED, LOUIS S. The extent of health insurance coverage in the United States. Washington, U.S. Govt. Print. Off., 1965. 67p. (Research report no. 10)
Describes data from health insurance organizations and from household surveys and compares the findings.

———. Financial experience of health insurance organizations in the United States. Washington, U.S. Govt. Print. Off., 1966. 64p. (Research report no. 12)
Provides an analysis of some of the factors which influence underwriting experience, and comparisons among the different types of organizations.

———. Private health insurance: coverage and financial experience, 1940–66. *Social Security Bulletin,* v. 30, November 1967: 3–22.

———. and KATHLEEN MYERS. Health insurance coverage complementary to Medicare. *Social Security Bulletin,* v. 30, August 1967: 3–14.
Describes the coverage offered by the various types of health insurance organizations.

———. *and others.* Independent health insurance plans in the United States; 1965 survey. Washington, U.S. Govt. Print. Off., 1966. 98p. (Research report no. 17)
All health insurance plans and organizations other than Blue Cross-Blue Shield and insurance companies.

RICE, DOROTHY P. Estimating the cost of illness. *American Journal of Public Health,* v. 57, March 1967: 424–440.
Outlines a methodological framework for calculating single-year costs of illness, disability and death.

RICE, DOROTHY P., and LOUCELE A. HOROWITZ. Trends in medical care prices. *Social Security Bulletin,* v. 30, July 1967: 13–27.

Describes in detail the trends in medical care prices since World War II, with special reference to their growth since the end of 1965.

SASULY, RICHARD, and MILTON I. ROEMER. Health insurance patterns: a conceptualization from the California scene. *Journal of Health and Human Behavior,* v. 7, Spring 1966: 36–44.

SCHEIDEMANDEL, PATRICIA, *and others.* Health insurance for mental illness. Washington, Joint Information Service of the American Psychiatric Association and the National Association for Mental Health, 1968. 89p.

Traces growth of health insurance coverage for mental illness, compares mental illness coverage with coverage for other illnesses, and includes data on insurance coverage of psychiatric patients in selected hospitals and in offices of psychiatrists in private practice.

SELDOWITZ, ESTELLE, and AGNES W. BREWSTER. Sweden's health and cash sickness insurance program. *Public Health Reports,* v. 79, September 1964: 815–822.

Provisions, costs, and benefits under the 1963 National Insurance Act.

SHAPIRO, SAM, *and others.* Patterns of medical use by the indigent aged under two systems of medical care. *American Journal of Public Health,* v. 57, May 1967: 784–790.

Analyzes the experience of New York City welfare clients enrolled with seven HIP groups and of those receiving care from other sources.

SNOKE, ALBERT W. Medicare year one: a critical appraisal. *Hospitals,* v. 41, November 1, 1967: 49–53.

A hospital administrator discusses the effects of Medicare on hospitals and on individual patients.

SOMERS, HERMAN M. Financing of medical care in the United States. *New England Journal of Medicine,* v. 275, Sept. 29, 1966: 702–709.

Discusses both private and public financing.

——. and ANNE RAMSAY SOMERS. Medicare and the hospitals; issues and prospects. Washington, Brookings, 1967. 303p.

Defines, analyzes, and evaluates: hospital organization, financing, staffing, planning, quality controls and cost controls; and Medicare's influence on these and other aspects of health care, including physicians' services.

STEWART, WILLIAM H. The positive impact of Medicare on the nation's health care systems. *Social Security Bulletin,* v. 30, July 1967: 9–12; 50.

What Medicare has accomplished, the trends that are emerging and new opportunities that exist today as a result of this program.

TOMES, IGOR. Basic features of sickness insurance in European socialist countries. *International Labour Review*, v. 93, March 1967: 202–214.
Covers Bulgaria, Czechoslovakia, the German Democratic Republic, Hungary, Poland, Rumania and the U.S.S.R.

TROAN, JOHN. What you've got coming from medicare and social security. Rev. ed. New York, Pocket Books, 1966. 80p.

U.S. BOARD OF TRUSTEES OF THE FEDERAL HOSPITAL INSURANCE TRUST FUND. Annual report. Washington, U.S. Govt. Print. Off.

U.S. BOARD OF TRUSTEES OF THE FEDERAL SUPPLEMENTARY MEDICAL INSURANCE TRUST FUND. Annual report. Washington, U.S. Govt. Print. Off.

U.S. BUREAU OF LABOR STATISTICS. Digest of 100 selected health and insurance plans under collective bargaining, early 1966. Washington, U.S. Govt. Print. Off., 1966. 152p. (Bulletin no. 1502)

U.S. CONGRESS. SENATE. SPECIAL COMMITTEE ON AGING. Blue Cross and private health insurance coverage of older Americans. Washington, U.S. Govt. Print. Off., 1964. 153p. (88th Cong., 2d sess., committee print)
Effort to determine the present and potential ability of the private health insurance industry to meet the health care financing needs of the elderly.

————. ————. ————. Health insurance and related provisions of P.L. 89–97, the social security amendments of 1965. Washington, U.S. Govt. Print. Off., 1965. 68p. (89th Cong., 1st sess., committee print)

U.S. DEPT. OF HEALTH, EDUCATION, AND WELFARE. A report to the President on medical care prices. Washington, U.S. Govt. Print. Off., 1967. 38p.
Reasons behind the rapid rise in the price of medical care with recommendations for moderating the rise.

U.S. SOCIAL SECURITY ADMINISTRATION. Directory of providers of services; extended care facilities, Title XVIII. 2d ed. Washington, U.S. Govt. Print. Off., 1967. Various paging.
Names and addresses of extended care facilities which are participating as providers of services in the Health Insurance for the Aged Program.

————. Directory of providers of services; home health agencies, Title XVIII. 2d ed. Washington, U.S. Govt. Print. Off., 1967. Various paging.
Names and addresses of home health agencies which are participating as providers of services in the Health Insurance for the Aged Program.

U.S. SOCIAL SECURITY ADMINISTRATION. Directory of providers of services; hospitals, Title XVIII. Washington, U.S. Govt. Print. Off., 1967. Various paging.

> Names and addresses of hospitals which are participating as providers of services in the Health Insurance for the Aged Program.

————. Directory of suppliers of services; independent laboratories, Title XVIII. Washington, U.S. Govt. Print. Off., 1967. Various paging.

> Names and addresses of independent laboratories which are participating as suppliers of services in the Health Insurance for the Aged Program.

Voluntary organizations in medical care planning. *American Journal of Public Health,* v. 54, March 1964: 447–460.

> Views of labor, management and hospitals; role of group practice; community hospital planning associations; voluntary action and the planning process.

WEBBER, IRVING L., ed. Medical care under social security; potentials and problems. Gainesville, University of Florida Press, 1966. 138p. (Institute of Gerontology series no. 15)

> Report on the 15th annual Southern Conference on Gerontology held at the University of Florida, February 14–15, 1966.

WEST, HOWARD. Health insurance for the aged: the statistical program. *Social Security Bulletin,* v. 30, January 1967: 3–16.

> Briefly describes provisions of the program, outlines the various components of the statistical system for collection and maintenance of data, and delineates the analytical studies envisioned.

WICKMAN, J. M. Evaluating the health insurance risk. Cincinnati, National Underwriter Co., 1965, 248p.

> Handbook for evaluating medical histories and other factors.

OASDHI and Related Programs

ALTMEYER, ARTHUR J. The formative years of social security. Madison, University of Wisconsin Press, 1966. 314p.

> Background for the passage of the Social Security Act and for the growth and administration of the program from 1934 to 1954.

BALL, ROBERT M. Policy issues in social security. *Social Security Bulletin,* v. 29, June 1966: 3–9.

> Major characteristics and level of accomplishment of the present social security system and policy issues involved.

BAYO, FRANCISCO, and MILTON P. GLANZ. Mortality experience of workers entitled to old-age benefits under OASDI, 1941–1961. Washington, U.S. Social Security Administration, Division of the Actuary, 1965. 35p. (Actuarial study no. 60)

Study limited to workers entitled to a retirement benefit on their own earnings record.

COHEN, WILBUR J., *and others.* Social security payments to noninsured persons. *Social Security Bulletin,* v. 29, September 1966: 3–9.

Background, legislative history, and summary of main provisions of the Tax Adjustment Act of 1966 which includes amendments affecting the social security program.

————. and ROBERT M. BALL. Social security amendments of 1965; summary and legislative history. *Social Security Bulletin,* v. 28, Sept. 1965: 3–21.

DEL POZO, EFREN C. The Mexican Institute for Social Security. *American Journal of Public Health,* v. 55, December 1965: 1957–1963.

Comprehensive survey of the Mexican social security program with emphasis on its medical aspects.

DOUBLET, JACQUES. Supplementary pension schemes in France. *Bulletin of the International Social Security Association,* v. 18, October 1965: 447–463.

Describes supplementary social security schemes in France.

Dual beneficiaries under Railroad Retirement and Social Security Acts, 1962. *Monthly Review* (Railroad Retirement Board), v. 26, March 1965: 2–6; 13.

Summarizes information on dual beneficiaries as of the end of 1962.

EPSTEIN, LENORE A. Workers entitled to minimum retirement benefits under OASDHI. *Social Security Bulletin,* v. 30, March 1967: 3–13.

Characteristics and resources of workers whose earnings qualified them for the minimum primary insurance amount.

FISHER, PAUL. Old-age and sickness insurance in West Germany in 1965. Washington, U.S. Govt. Print. Off., 1965. 56p. (Research report no. 13)

Examines current issues, analyzes experience with semi-automatic adjustment of pensions to wage-level changes, and highlights some aspects of Germany's sickness insurance.

GERIG, DANIEL S. Social security in the new African countries. *Social Security Bulletin,* v. 29, January 1966: 29–44.

Reviews present status of social security measures and some aspects of their probable development.

————. and ROBERT J. MYERS. Canada Pension Plan of 1965. *Social Security Bulletin,* v. 28, November 1965: 3–17.

Similarities and differences between the Canadian system and that of the U.S.

71

HART, MARICE C. Railroad Retirement Act as amended in 1965. *Social Security Bulletin,* v. 29, February 1966: 26–38.

Discusses major provisions, legislative development and relationship between railroad retirement and OASDHI.

HASENBERG, WERNER. Income-tax treatment of old-age pensions and contributions here and abroad. *Social Security Bulletin,* v. 29, August 1966: 10–18.

Results of a study of available information on the income-tax treatment of benefits and contributions under old-age pension programs in 22 countries.

HIGUCHI, T. Old-age pensions and retirement. *International Labour Review,* v. 90, October 1964: 333–351.

Analyzes general old-age schemes of 40 countries, and standards laid down in international labor conventions and recommendations.

HOGARTH, JAMES. The payment of the physician; some European comparisons. New York, Macmillan, 1963. 684p.

Comparative study of methods of remuneration of the physician in publicly organized, or publicly sponsored, medical service.

HOLTZMAN, ABRAHAM. The Townsend movement; a political study. New York, Bookman Associates, 1963. 256p.

Documented analysis of the movement started by Dr. Francis Townsend to help other people before the passage of the Social Security Act.

INTERNATIONAL SOCIAL SECURITY ASSOCIATION. GENERAL ASSEMBLY. Reports. Geneva, Secretariat General of the I.S.S.A.

JAPAN. SOCIAL INSURANCE AGENCY. Outline of social insurance in Japan. Tokyo, 1966. 75p.

JOHNSEN, JULIA E., comp. Selected articles on social insurance. New York, H. W. Wilson, 1922. 381p.

Debater's handbook presenting pros and cons on: workmen's compensation; health, maternity, old age, and invalidity insurance; benefits to widows and orphans; soldiers and sailors insurance.

KANEV, ITZHAK, and ARGEH NIZAN. Public expenditures on social security and social services in Israel and international comparisons (1961/62–1962/63). Tel Aviv, Social and Economic Research Institute and the Research Department of Kupat-Holim, 1966. 102p.

KEWELY, THOMAS H. Social security in Australia. Sydney, Sydney University Press, 1965. 401p.

Development of social security from 1900 to the present.

KRISLOV, JOSEPH. State and local government retirement systems . . . 1965. Washington, U.S. Govt. Print. Off., 1966. 82p. (Research report no. 15)

A survey of systems covering employees also covered by the federal old-age, survivors, disability, and health insurance program.

LUBOVE, ROY. The struggle for social security, 1900–1935. Cambridge, Mass., Harvard University Press, 1968. 276p.

Comprehensive study of the evolution of the social security concept in the United States up to the New Deal.

MAISONPIERRE, ANDRE. Social insurance in Britain and Sweden. *Journal of American Insurance,* v. 43, May-June 1967: 13–15.

Shortcomings of two systems.

MESSER, ELIZABETH F. "Thirty-eight years is a plenty." *Civil Service Journal,* v. 5, October-December 1964: 6–8; 20–24.

Responses to a Civil Service Commission questionnaire about early retirement, with a statistical summary of answers to the key questions.

MYERS, ROBERT J. Actuarial cost estimates for Hospital Insurance Act of 1965 and Social Security Amendments of 1965. Washington, U.S. Social Security Administration, Division of the Actuary, 1965. 54p. (Actuarial study no. 59)

Revision and expansion of actuarial studies nos. 52 and 57, and also presents cost estimates for proposed changes in the cash benefits program.

———. Social insurance and allied government programs. Homewood, Ill., Irwin, 1965. 258p.

Forty-eight page addendum summarizes the Social Security Amendments of 1965, by program, with respect to major changes made.

———. and FRANCISCO BAYO. Hospital insurance, supplementary medical insurance, and old-age, survivors, and disability insurance financing basis under the 1965 amendments. *Social Security Bulletin,* v. 28, October 1965: 17–28.

———. ———. Long-range cost estimates for old-age, survivors, and disability insurance system, 1966. Washington, U.S. Social Security Administration, Office of the Actuary, 1967. 47p. (Actuarial study no. 63)

Estimates relate to the OASDI cash-benefits program as it was after the 1965 amendments, valued as of January 1, 1967.

———. ———. Old-age, survivors, and disability insurance: administrative expenses. *Social Security Bulletin,* v. 29, July 1966: 3–8.

Describes how the costs of administering the old-age, survivors, and disability program are met.

NATIONAL CONFERENCE ON SOCIAL SECURITY. Report of proceedings. New York, American Association for Social Security, Inc.

First conference held in 1928. First five conference proceedings bore the title: "Old age security in the United States." Sixth through the fourteenth proceedings were titled: "Social security in the United States." Last conference held in 1941.

NIESSEN, A. M. Tenth actuarial valuation of the assets and liabilities under the Railroad Retirement Acts as of December 31, 1965, with technical supplement. Chicago, U.S. Railroad Retirement Board, 1968. 120p.

NORWAY. NATIONAL INSURANCE INSTITUTION. The Norwegian system of social insurance; a survey. Oslo, 1966. 65p.

Includes tabular survey of social insurance schemes.

PALMORE, ERDMAN, and others. Widows with children under social security. Washington, U.S. Govt. Print. Off., 1966. 96p. (Research report no. 16)

1963 National Survey of Widows with Children under OASDHI.

A plan for social security reform in Italy. *International Labour Review,* v. 91, February 1965: 121–134.

Reviews existing Italian social security schemes and sets forth proposals and recommendations adopted by the National Economic and Labour Council (C.N.E.L.).

POLINSKY, ELLA J. Women household workers covered by old-age, survivors, and disability insurance. *Social Security Bulletin,* v. 28, July 1965: 33–38.

Age, race, length of coverage, and annual income.

ROBB, A. C. The impact of state pensions on public service superannuation schemes. *Journal of the Institute of Actuaries,* v. 91, Pt. II, no. 389, 1965: 147–171.

Considers the impact of a further expansion of the National Insurance Scheme, which may lead to future changes in public service schemes.

RUBIN, HAROLD. Pensions and employee mobility in the public service. New York, Twentieth Century Fund, 1965. 105p.

Study based primarily on a mail survey of federal, state, and local governments.

SCHEWE, DIETER. Old-age and survivors' protection for the self-employed: an international comparison. *International Labour Review,* v. 91, January 1965: 1–13.

Does not include developing countries.

SCHORR, ALVIN L. Social security and social services in France. Washington, U.S. Govt. Print. Off., 1965. 48p. (Research report no. 7)
French social security as an organic entity; family unions; evaluation of the effects of social services and social security upon each other.

SEAGER, HENRY ROGERS. Social insurance, a program of social reform. New York, Macmillan, 1910. 175p.
The Kennedy lectures for 1910, in the School of Philanthropy, conducted by the Charity Organization Society of the City of New York.

SOCIAL INSURANCE FUNDS OF PERU. Social security in Peru. *Bulletin of the International Social Security Association,* v. 16, August-September 1963: 221–265.
History and provisions of social security legislation in Peru.

Social security in the U.S.S.R. *Bulletin of the International Social Security Association,* v. 17, August-September 1964: 217–271.

U.S. ADVISORY COUNCIL ON SOCIAL SECURITY. The status of the social security program and recommendations for its improvement. Report. Washington, 1965. 115p.

U.S. ADVISORY COUNCIL ON SOCIAL SECURITY FINANCING. Financing old-age, survivors, and disability insurance. A report. Washington, U.S. Govt. Print. Off., 1959. 30p.
Findings and recommendations.

U.S. BOARD OF TRUSTEES OF THE FEDERAL OLD-AGE AND SURVIVORS INSURANCE TRUST FUND AND THE FEDERAL DISABILITY TRUST FUND. Annual report. Washington, U.S. Govt. Print. Off.

U.S. BUREAU OF LABOR STATISTICS. Public old-age pensions and insurance in the United States and in foreign countries. Washington, U.S. Govt. Print. Off., 1932. 367p. (U.S. Bureau of Labor Statistics Bulletin no. 561)

———. Public service retirement systems; United States, Canada and Europe. Washington, U.S. Govt. Print. Off., 1929. 223p. (U.S. Bureau of Labor Statistics Bulletin no. 477)

U.S. CONGRESS. HOUSE. COMMITTEE ON WAYS AND MEANS. Actuarial cost estimates and summary of provisions of the old-age, survivors, and disability insurance system as modified by the Social Security Amendments of 1965, and actuarial cost estimates and summary of provisions of the hospital insurance and supplementary medical insurance systems as established by such act. Washington, U.S. Govt. Print. Off., 1965. 51p. (89th Cong., 1st sess., committee print)

75

U.S. Congress. House. Committee on Ways and Means. Section-by-section analysis and explanation of provisions of H.R. 5710, the "Social Security Amendments of 1967," as introduced on February 20, 1967. Washington, U.S. Govt. Print. Off., 1967. 44p. (90th Cong., 1st sess., committee print)

Prepared by the U.S. Dept. of Health, Education, and Welfare.

———. Joint Economic Committee. European social security systems; a comparative analysis of programs in England, Sweden, and the Common Market countries, together with a description of the U.S. system. Washington, U.S. Govt. Print. Off., 1965. 129p. (Economic policies and practices paper no. 7) (89th Cong., 1st sess., joint committee print)

U.S. Railroad Retirement Board. Annual report. Washington, U.S. Govt. Print. Off.

U.S. Social Security Administration. Social security handbook on retirement insurance, survivors insurance, disability insurance, health insurance for the aged. 3rd ed. Washington, U.S. Govt. Print. Off., 1966. 461p.

Provisions of the Social Security Act as amended through April 1966, regulations, and brief descriptions of other related benefit programs.

———. Office of Research and Statistics. Annual statistical supplement to the *Social Security Bulletin*. Washington, U.S. Govt. Print. Off.

Calendar-year and trend data for social security and related programs.

———. ———. Social security farm statistics, 1955–1963: farmers and farm workers under Old-Age, Survivors, Disability, and Health Insurance. Washington, 1966. 34p.

Selected statistics on hired farm workers and self-employed farmers with coverage under the Social Security Act.

———. ———. Social security programs throughout the world, 1967. Washington, U.S. Govt. Print. Off., 1967. 239p.

Complete revision of previous publications dealing with foreign social security systems.

Vaughan, Emmett J. Social insurance in Yugoslavia. *Journal of Risk and Insurance,* v. 32, September 1965: 385–393.

Waldman, Saul. OASDI benefits, prices, and wages: 1966 experience. *Social Security Bulletin,* v. 30, June 1967: 9–12; 36.

Background information for use by those considering the problems of benefit adequacy.

———. Retirement systems for employees of state and local governments . . . 1966; findings of a survey of systems whose members were not covered under the OASDHI program. Washington, U.S. Govt. Print. Off., 1968. 115p. (Research report no. 23)

WALDMAN, SAUL. State and local government retirement systems, 1966: provisions for employees not under OASDHI. *Social Security Bulletin,* v. 30, September 1967: 3–11; 43.

Summary of the findings of the 1966 survey of the state and local government retirement systems whose members are not covered under OASDHI.

Private Pension Systems and Retirement Policies

BANKERS TRUST COMPANY, NEW YORK. 1965 study of industrial retirement plans; including analyses of complete programs recently adopted or revised. New York, 1965. 263p.

BEATTIE, ORVILLE C., and DONALD I. BROTHERS. Changes in the wind for pension funds. *Management Review,* v. 56, May 1967: 10–18.

Discusses six areas of concern and presents various alternatives for fulfilling public objectives.

BEIER, EMERSON H. Terminations of pension plans: 11 years' experience. *Monthly Labor Review,* v. 90, June 1967: 26–30.

Causes and effects of termination and characteristics of plans closed out between 1955 and 1965.

BERGEN, JOSEPH S. Balanced pensions compared with variable plans— historical examples. *Pension and Welfare News,* v. 4, December 1967: 30–35.

BERNSTEIN, MERTON C. The future of private pensions. New York, Free Press, 1964. 385p.

Analyzes the purposes of private pension plans and their resultant effectiveness.

BIEGEL, HERMAN C., *and others.* Pensions and profit sharing. 3rd ed. Washington, BNA Inc., 1964. 283p.

Private pension plans in business and industry.

BROWN, ROBERT E. Retirement plans for the self-employed. *Journal of the American Society of Chartered Life Underwriters,* v. 20, Summer 1966: 237–252.

Summarizes the Self-Employed Individual's Retirement Act of 1962, evaluates the legislation, and makes recommendations for changes.

BURRALL, CHARLES L., JR. Recent developments in church pension plans. *Pension and Welfare News,* v. 3, March 1967: 39–40; 54.

Historical sketch and brief survey of recent developments.

CLARK, HAROLD A. Retirement income goals. *Journal of the American Society of Chartered Life Underwriters,* v. 19, Fall 1965: 307–318.

Discusses retirement planning in relation to private and public retirement systems.

CLARKE, L. SHELTON, JR. A dynamic pension market with commentary on the President's committee pension report. *Journal of the American Society of Chartered Life Underwriters,* v. 19, Fall 1965: 293–306.

Discusses expected changes in pension law, based on the report of the President's Committee on Corporate Pension Funds.

CRAMER, JOE J., JR. "Unrealized" appreciation and private pension plans. *Business Horizons,* v. 8, Fall 1965: 87–95.

Methods of asset valuation with a recommendation of one method in particular.

FOOTE, GEORGE H., and DAVID J. McLAUGHLIN. The president's stake in pension planning. *Harvard Business Review,* v. 43, September-October 1965: 91–106.

Survey of retirement programs of 490 large corporations.

FOSTER, CLARK T., and BARNET N. BERIN. What is your pension plan worth? *Pension and Welfare News,* v. 4, December 1967: 23–26; 39.

Describes a flexible method for pension plan valuation.

FOX, HARLAND. Top executive pensions, 1957 and 1963. *Conference Board Record,* v. 1, October 1964: 7–10.

Median benefit in manufacturing has risen from 28% of salary in 1957 to 34% of salary in 1963.

―――. The widow's pension. *Conference Board Record,* v. 1, May 1964: 38–44.

Preretirement death benefit funded under individual insurance contracts.

FROEBIG, WILLIAM F. Self-administered trusteed pension plans. *Journal of the American Society of Chartered Life Underwriters,* v. 20, Summer 1966: 269–287.

Analysis of the self-administered trusteed method for financing private pension plans.

GREENOUGH, WILLIAM C. The potential of the private pension system. *Best's Insurance News,* life edition, v. 68, November 1967: 40–46.

What federal and state governments can do through indirect action.

HINCKLEY, CHARLES C. Self-employed retirement plans. *CLU Journal,* v. 21, October 1967: 25–33.

Discusses mathematics of participation in qualified self-employed retirement plans, the whys and wherefores of life insurance in these plans, and the problems and planning techniques.

HOLLAND, DANIEL M. Private pension funds: projected growth. New York, Columbia University Press, 1966. 146p. (National Bureau of Economic Research, Occasional Paper no. 97)

HUBBARD, RUSSELL H., JR. The future of private pension plans. *Financial Executive*, v. 35, April 1967: 30–40.

Reviews opportunities to strengthen the private pension plan system and the obstacles that must be overcome.

HUDEK, PAUL R. Loss of pension benefits through termination of private pension plans—an actuarial analysis. *Pension and Welfare News*, v. 4, December 1967: 36–39.

Supplements conclusions drawn by Emerson H. Beier in his article in the June 1967 issue of the *Monthly Labor Review*.

INSTITUTE OF LIFE INSURANCE. Private and public pension plans in the United States. New York, 1967. 28p.

Brief history of the development of pension plans, with comprehensive statistics for the various types to show coverage, retirement income, costs to employers and employees, and their role in the capital market.

KEENE, KENNETH K. Insured vs. trusteed pension programs. *Journal of the American Society of Chartered Life Underwriters*, v. 19, Winter 1965: 35–45.

Emphasis on investment results.

KOLODRUBETZ, WALTER W. Growth in employee-benefit plans, 1950–1965. *Social Security Bulletin*, v. 30, April 1967: 10–27.

Discusses trends, developments and innovations in plans sponsored and underwritten by private organizations for employees and their families for old-age, death, disability, unemployment, and the cost of medical care.

LANDAY, DONALD M. Private pension plan coverage of older workers. *Monthly Labor Review*, v. 90, August 1967: 47–51.

Significant facts from a special survey of pension plan coverage of wage and salary workers age 50 to 64 years in private nonfarm jobs made in January 1966.

LATIMER, MURRAY WEBB. Industrial pension systems in the United States and Canada. New York, Industrial Relations Counselors, Inc., 1932. 2 v.

———. Trade union pension systems, and other superannuation and total disability in the United States and Canada. New York, Industrial Relations Counselors, Inc., 1932. 205p.

LUCAS, VANE B., JR. Private pension issues under collective bargaining. *Journal of Risk and Insurance*, v. 32, December 1965: 549–558.

General discussion of bargaining issues.

MCGINN, DANIEL F. A case for portable pensions. *Best's Insurance News*, life edition, v. 66, December 1965: 67–70; 73.

Discusses what must be done if portability is to be made a nationwide feature of private pension plans.

Mandatory retirement regulations for classroom teachers, 308 local school systems. *Educational Research Service Circular,* no. 4, 1965, June 1965. 20p.

Results of a questionnaire sent out in December 1963 to more than 400 school systems with enrollments of 12,000 or more.

MARPLES, WILLIAM F. Actuarial aspects of pension security. Homewood, Ill., Irwin, 1965. 210p.

MATHIASEN, GENEVA, ed. Criteria for retirement. A report of a national conference on retirement of older workers. New York, Putnam, 1953. 233p.

Premise of the conference was that chronological age has not proved acceptable as a sole basis for retirement policy.

————. Flexible retirement; evolving policies and programs for industry and labor. New York, Putnam, 1959. 226p.

MAYERSON, ALLEN L. Financing private pension plans in the United States. *International Review on Actuarial and Statistical Problems of Social Security,* no. 9, 1963: 11–30.

MELONE, JOSEPH J., and EVERETT T. ALLEN, JR. Pension planning; pensions, profit sharing and other deferred compensation plans. Homewood, Ill., Dow-Jones-Irwin, 1967. 404p.

Broad actuarial, legal (tax), and administrative aspects.

MYERS, ROBERT J. The mine workers' welfare and retirement fund: fifteen years' experience. *Industrial and Labor Relations Review,* v. 20, January 1967: 265–274.

Analyzes the operating experience of the United Mine Workers of America Welfare and Retirement Fund during 1961–1965, with emphasis given to the financial condition of the fund.

————. Variable income pension plan of the Lutheran Church in America. *Pension and Welfare News,* v. 3, February 1967: 46–47.

Describes the variable-income alternative basis for the Lutheran Church in America's pension plans for ministers and lay employees.

NATIONAL FOUNDATION OF HEALTH, WELFARE AND PENSION PLANS. Comparing and appraising investment performance of pension plans. Milwaukee, 1967. 80p. (Part II of research project no. 1)

Describes and illustrates techniques for making valid comparisons of the investment performance of different pension funds.

NATIONAL INDUSTRIAL CONFERENCE BOARD. Industrial pensions in the United States. New York, 1925. 157p.

Panel discussion—insurance and pension plans for retired persons. *Journal of the American Geriatrics Society,* v. 14, April 1966: 309–325.

Present or pending government programs not discussed except as they directly affect the factual data presented.

PARKER, FLORENCE EVELYN. Beneficial activities of American trade unions. Washington, U.S. Govt. Print. Off., 1928. 229p. (Bureau of Labor Statistics Bulletin no. 465)

PATTERSON, EDWIN W. Legal protection of private pension expectations. Homewood, Ill., Irwin, 1960. 286p.
Critical inquiry, inaugurated by the Pension Research Council of the Wharton School of Finance and Commerce of the University of Pennsylvania, into the factual basis of benefit expectations under private pension plans.

PETERSON, RAY M. The future of private pension plans. *Journal of Risk and Insurance,* v. 33, December 1966: 603–620.

PILCH, MICHAEL, and VICTOR WOOD. New trends in pensions. London, Hutchinson, 1964. 223p.
Based on a survey of 180 companies.

————. ————. Pension scheme practice. London, Hutchinson, 1967. 192p.
Intended for the layman who wants up-to-date and factual guidance.

Retirement statistics, 1964. *NEA Research Bulletin,* v. 42, December 1964: 99–107.
Changes in teacher retirement plans since 1950.

ROMM, ELLIOT. Pension planning: a data book. New York, American Management Association, 1960. 79p. (AMA Research Study no. 43)
Study of the characteristics of 127 company retirement plans.

SCHULTZ, E. B. The TVA preretirement program. Washington, U.S. Govt. Print. Off., 1961. 18p. (Patterns for progress in aging, case study no. 9)
Prepared under the direction of the Special Staff on Aging of the U.S. Department of Health, Education, and Welfare.

SHIELD, W. LEE, and ARTHUR S. FEFFERMAN. The challenge to the private pension system. *Journal of the American Society of Chartered Life Underwriters,* v. 20, Summer 1966: 197–214.
Discusses suggestions to improve the pension system and issues involved in proposals to establish new institutions in the pension area.

SKOLNIK, ALFRED M. Ten years of employee-benefit plans. *Social Security Bulletin,* v. 29, April 1966: 3–19.
Analyzes statistical data on employee-benefit plans and discusses trends in the field of private pension plans.

SLAVICK, FRED. Compulsory and flexible retirement in the American economy. Ithaca, N.Y., Cornell University, 1966. 172p.

Analysis of the plant and establishment characteristics associated with the use of compulsory and flexible retirement policies, and including estimates of the prevalence of the various types of policies in 1962.

SQUIER, LEE WELLING. Old age dependency in the United States; a complete survey of the pension movement. New York, Macmillan, 1912. 361p.

Reviews causes of old age dependency, efforts at relief, and plans for prevention.

A symposium: early retirement. *Industrial Relations,* v. 4, May 1965: 1–60.

Articles by: *Max D. Kossoris, Charles E. Odell, Merton C. Bernstein, Melvin K. Bers,* and *Ralph and Estelle James.*

TARVER, NORMAN H. The future of private pension plans. *Pension and Welfare News,* v. 3, August 1967: 22–28.

Study of three papers presented at a January 1967 meeting sponsored by the American Management Association, of two statements by *Senator Jacob Javits,* and of a paper by *Assistant Secretary of the Treasury Stanley S. Surrey.*

TOMES, IGOR. Problems of retirement age and related conditions for the receipt of old-age benefits (comparative study). Geneva, International Social Security Association, 1966. Various paging.

Trends in retirement planning; TIAA–CREF: 1940 to 1964. *AAUP Bulletin,* v. 50, December 1964: 342–346.

Three main provisions under TIAA and CREF annuity contracts that vary from college to college.

TYSON, ROBERT C. Private pension plans and public policy. *Financial Executive,* v. 35, November 1967: 16–22.

Compares social security and private pension plans and warns of overregulation and increasing costs.

U.S. BUREAU OF LABOR STATISTICS. Labor mobility and private pension plans; a study of vesting, early retirement, and portability provisions. Washington, U.S. Govt. Print. Off., 1964. 74p. (BLS Bulletin no. 1407)

Describes the private pension plan structure, and sets forth the implications for labor mobility inherent in the provisions and practices.

——. Private pension plan benefits. Washington, U.S. Govt. Print. Off., 1966. 104p. (Bulletin no. 1485)

Deals with types and levels of benefits available for normal, disability, and early retirement. Also covers vesting provisions, supplementary pension plans, and death benefits.

U.S. CONGRESS. SENATE. SPECIAL COMMITTEE ON AGING. Extending private pension coverage; a report. Washington, U.S. Govt. Print. Off., 1965. 18p. (89th Cong., 1st sess., committee print)

Recommendations for providing added retirement incomes for older Americans.

U.S. PRESIDENT'S COMMITTEE ON CORPORATE PENSION FUNDS AND OTHER PRIVATE RETIREMENT AND WELFARE PROGRAMS. Public policy and private pension programs; a report to the President on private employee retirement plans. Washington, U.S. Govt. Print. Off., 1965. 82p.

Explores the place of private plans in the nation's economic security system and suggests ways by which these plans can function more effectively.

WILLIAMS, WALTER. The implications of retirement security systems for consumer behavior. *Journal of Risk and Insurance,* v. 32, September 1965: 349–366.

Effects of public, private, and OASDI retirement programs upon the propensity to consume, both of individuals currently receiving benefit payments and those not yet retired.

Public Assistance and Medicaid

ABBOTT, EDITH. Public assistance. Chicago, University of Chicago Press, 1940. 894p.

Uses selected documents, arranged in chronological order, to show the basic principles and policies of the public assistance systems up to the enactment of the social security program.

ABBOTT, GRACE. From relief to social security: the development of the new public welfare services and their administration. Chicago, University of Chicago Press, 1941. 388p.

Collection of papers, written during 1929–1939, which discuss early relief programs and the Social Security Act.

ADAMS, MARGARET K. Medical assistance for the aged; state legislation in 1965. *Welfare in Review,* v. 4, October 1966: 22–24.

AMERICAN PUBLIC WELFARE ASSOCIATION. The patient comes first in medical assistance administration. Chicago, 1962. 42p.

Six papers presented at the 1961 biennial round table.

―――. Selected biennial round table conference papers, 1963. Chicago, 1964. 133p.

Papers on dependency, medical assistance, community planning, and protective services.

―――. MEDICAL ASSISTANCE RESEARCH PROJECT. Public assistance medical care: areas of needed research and an annotated bibliography. Chicago, 1959. 63p.

AMERICAN PUBLIC WELFARE ASSOCIATION. PROJECT ON AGING. Program planning for strengthening services to the aging through public welfare agencies. Chicago, 1965. 43p.
Guidelines developed in two seminars.

——. PUBLIC WELFARE PROJECT ON AGING. Agency self-evaluation guides for serving older people. Chicago, 1965. 72p.
Guide for exploring the needs of older people.

——. ——. Aging; progressive programing. Chicago, 1960. 41p.

——. ——. Local board members: partners in public welfare services to the aging. Chicago, 1963. 33p.
Report of two seminars held Dec. 13–14, 1962; and March 7–8, 1963.

——. ——. Medical care for the aging; public welfare's administrative role. Chicago, 1963. 31p.
Report of a seminar dealing with the administrative aspects of the provision of medical care services for the aging through state and local public welfare agencies.

——. ——. Public relations focuses on aging. Chicago, 1962. 28p.
Proceedings of a seminar for selected public relations and public information specialists serving State and local public welfare departments to help the agencies expand and improve programs designed to meet social, economic, and health needs for the aging.

——. ——. Rural public welfare administration of services for the aging. Chicago, 1962. 26p.
Seminar for selected administrators of local rural areas to help State and local public welfare agencies expand and improve programs designed to meet social, economic and health needs of the aging.

BORNET, VAUGHN DAVIS. Welfare in America. Norman, University of Oklahoma Press, 1960. 319p.
Detailed analysis of public and private welfare in the United States.

BRECKINRIDGE, ELIZABETH. New directions in public welfare services for the aging. Chicago, American Public Welfare Association, 1955. 16p. (How public welfare serves aging people, no. 9)

BROWN, JOSEPHINE CHAPIN. Public relief 1929–1939. New York, Holt, 1940. 524p.

CALIFORNIA. LEGISLATURE. ASSEMBLY INTERIM COMMITTEE ON WAYS AND MEANS. Final report on health care services for the aged. Sacramento, Assembly of the State of California, 1965. 66p.
Description of the MAA program.

CLEGG, REED K. The administrator in public welfare. Springfield, Ill., Thomas, 1966. 271p.

Includes history of public welfare, the role of the government, public relations, staff development, and the future development of public welfare.

COUNCIL OF STATE GOVERNMENTS. State medical fee payments; procedure for setting and selecting schedules for public assistance and child welfare vendor payments. Chicago, 1967. 49p.

Information on procedures followed in the states for setting fees for vendor payment of medical goods and services.

EPPLEY, DAVID B. Concurrent receipt of public assistance and old-age, survivors, and disability insurance by persons aged 65 and over, early 1963. *Welfare in Review,* v. 2, March 1964: 18–23.

FRENCH, DAVID G., ed. Planning responsibilities of state departments of public welfare. Chicago, American Public Welfare Association, 1967. 82p.

Conference co-sponsored by the American Public Welfare Association Project on Aging and the Florence Heller Graduate School for Advanced Studies in Social Welfare.

HAUGHTON, JAMES G. Quality control in public welfare medical care. *Public Welfare,* v. 24, October 1966: 267–273.

Goals for the new medical assistance program (title XIX).

HENDERSON, GEORGE. The Negro recipient of old-age assistance: results of discrimination. *Social Casework,* v. 46, April 1965: 208–214.

Discusses factors that seem unique to 100 aged Negroes who were recipients of OAA grants.

HUNT, MAURICE O. The range of public welfare services to older people. Chicago, American Public Welfare Association, 1954. 15p. (How public welfare serves aging people, no. 1)

LEYENDECKER, HILARY M. Problems and policy in public assistance. New York, Harper, 1955. 400p.

Considers the development, general characteristics, organization, and administration of public assistance.

LOTWIN, GERTRUDE. A State revises its assistance standard. Washington, U.S. Govt. Print. Off., 1959. 40p. (Public Assistance Report no. 37)

Deals with the development of a defined standard of economic security which resulted in a less detailed procedure for workers in determining need and amounts of assistance under the State of New Jersey's program of public assistance.

MARTZ, HELEN E. Medical care for the aged under MAA and OAA, 1960–1963. *Welfare in Review,* v. 2, February 1964: 3–12.

Review of 3 years' experience.

MELLMAN, RICHARD J. Title XIX grants to states for medical assistance programs. *Pension and Welfare News,* v. 3, May 1967: 36–38.
Private health insurance versus governmental programs.

MUGGE, ROBERT H. Age variations in old-age assistance. *Welfare in Review,* v. 4, December 1966: 13–18.
Investigates the hypothesis that the nature and severity of problems vary by age for old-age assistance recipients.

O'REILLY, CHARLES T., and MARGARET M. PEMBROKE. OAA profile; the old age assistance client in Chicago. Chicago, Loyola University Press, 1961. 119p.
Excerpts from research reports of participants in a group research project.

SOUTHERN REGIONAL COUNCIL. Public assistance: to what end? Atlanta, Georgia, 1967. 41p.
Discusses what is needed to make an adequate program of public assistance.

STEINER, GILBERT Y. Social insecurity: the politics of welfare. Chicago, Rand McNally, 1966. 270p.
The political circumstances that produce a particular welfare policy, especially public assistance.

TAX FOUNDATION. Public assistance, a survey of selected aspects of state programs. New York, 1960. 64p. (Project note no. 46)
History, intergovernmental relationships, medical care aspects, costs and financing, and ways and means of safeguarding of public welfare programs.

TRECKER, HARLEIGH B. Group services in public welfare; guides for administration and program development. Washington, U.S. Govt. Print. Off., 1964. 65p. (P.A. report no. 55)

U.S. ADVISORY COUNCIL ON PUBLIC ASSISTANCE. Public assistance. A report. Washington, U.S. Govt. Print. Off., 1960. 137p. (86th Cong., 2nd sess., S. doc. 93)
Findings and recommendations.

U.S. ADVISORY COUNCIL ON PUBLIC WELFARE. "Having the power, we have the duty;" report to the Secretary of Health, Education, and Welfare. Washington, U.S. Govt. Print. Off., 1966. 148p.
Findings and recommendations with respect to the administration of the public assistance program.

U.S. BUREAU OF FAMILY SERVICES. Characteristics of state public assistance plans under the Social Security Act. General provisions—eligibility, assistance, administration. Washington, U.S. Govt. Print. Off., 1964. 116p. (Public assistance report no. 50)
State plans which were in effect April 30, 1964.

U.S. BUREAU OF FAMILY SERVICES. Characteristics of state public assistance plans under the Social Security Act. Provisions for medical and remedial care. Washington, U.S. Govt. Print. Off., 1964. 192p.

State plans which were in effect as of April 30, 1964.

————. Characteristics of state public assistance plans under the Social Security Act. Provisions for social services. Washington, U.S. Govt. Print. Off., 1965. 133p. (Public assistance report no. 53)

Based on approved state plan provisions in effect on June 30, 1965.

————. Public assistance in the counties of the United States, June 1960. Washington, 1963. 179p.

Includes recipient rates and average payments in old-age assistance.

————. Questions and answers on medical assistance. Washington, U.S. Govt. Print. Off., 1967. 20p. (BFS 13–29)

————. DIVISION OF MEDICAL CARE STANDARDS. Medical care in public assistance, guides and recommended standards; organization and administration. Washington, 1962. 26p.

U.S. BUREAU OF PUBLIC ASSISTANCE. Public assistance under the Social Security Act. Washington, U.S. Govt. Print. Off., 1961. 30p. (Public assistance report no. 47)

Describes State and Federal responsibility and gives legislative history of the provisions of the act.

————. Services for older people; role of the public assistance programs and of the Bureau of Public Assistance in relation to older persons. Washington, U.S. Govt. Print. Off., 1959. 27p. (Public assistance report no. 38)

U.S. CONGRESS. SENATE. SPECIAL COMMITTEE ON AGING. Medical assistance for the aged; the Kerr-Mills program, 1960–1963. Washington, U.S. Govt. Print. Off., 1963. 103p. (88th Cong., 1st sess., committee print)

A report by the Subcommittee on Health of the Elderly.

————. ————. ————. Performance of the states. Eighteen months of experience with the medical assistance for the aged (Kerr-Mills) program; a report. Washington, U.S. Govt. Print. Off., 1962. 86p. (87th Cong., 2d sess., committee print)

————. ————. ————. Services to the elderly on public assistance. Washington, U.S. Govt. Print. Off., 1966. 26p. (89th Cong., 2d sess., committee print)

Report by the Subcommittee on Federal, State, and Community Services.

U.S. MEDICAL SERVICES ADMINISTRATION. The role of state medical advisory committees in Medicaid (Title XIX). Washington, 1967. 8p.

Describes briefly the organization and effective use of advisory committees in the medicaid program.

U.S. PRESIDENT'S COUNCIL ON AGING. Federal payments to older persons in need of protection; a report of a survey and conference. Washinton, U.S. Govt. Print. Off., 1965. 66p.

Survey of federal agencies administering major benefit-paying programs.

U.S. SOCIAL AND REHABILITATION SERVICE. Findings of the 1965 survey of old-age assistance recipients: data by state and census division. Washington, 1967–1968. 3 pts.

Part I. Demographic and program characteristics. Part II. Data obtained by mail questionnaire. Part III. Financial circumstances.

WHITE, GLADYS O. Determining financial eligibility for medical assistance for the aged. *Welfare in Review,* v. 2, June 1964: 8–15.

Summarizes the financial eligibility requirements of state programs.

———. Meeting financial needs under old-age assistance. *Welfare in Review,* v. 1, December 1963: 1–6.

Describes process of determining need and discusses extent to which aged people have their needs met by public assistance payments.

WICKENDEN, ELIZABETH. The needs of older people and public welfare services to meet them; an analysis and description of public welfare experience. Chicago, American Public Welfare Association, 1953. 146p.

HEALTH
and MEDICAL
CARE

Home Care Programs

BRYANT, ZELLA. Report on nursing care of the sick at home in incorporated U.S. cities with population of 25,000 and over. Washington, U.S. Govt. Print. Off., 1962. 31p. (Public Health Service publication no. 901)

COMMUNITY COUNCIL OF GREATER NEW YORK. Home aide service needs of health agency clientele. New York, 1961. 53p.
> Subtitle: "A study of the need for services in the home among clients of hospital social service departments and other health agencies in New York City: November 1960."

ELCONIN, ANN F., *and others.* An organized hospital-based home care program. *American Journal of Public Health,* v. 54, July 1964: 1106–1117.
> Deals with specific diagnostic groupings, and the pertinent social, economic, ethnic, and religious factors that influence their care at home.

FERGUSON, MARION, and RUTH PHILLIPS. Availability of services for nursing care of the sick at home. Washington, U.S. Govt. Print. Off., 1964. 47p. (Public Health Service publication no. 1265)
> Report on publicized programs of nursing care of the sick at home on a continuing basis to all who need it.

Home care. *Inquiry,* v. 4, October 1967: entire issue.
> Cost savings through use of home care; overall cost of operating a home care program; types of diseases considered suitable for home care; acceptance of home care by doctors, hospitals, and patients; potentials and problems of setting up a home health program as a part of a prepaid group practice plan; the involvement of Blue Cross in home care.

LEVINE, RACHEL A. Treatment in the home. *Social Work,* v. 9, January 1964: 19–28.
> Experiment by the Mental Hygiene Clinic of Henry Street Settlement to bring mental health services to the low-income, multi-problem family.

LITTAUER, DAVID, *and others.* Home care. Chicago, American Hospital Association, 1961. 110p. (Hospital monograph series no. 9)
> Describes organization and operation of a typical hospital-based home care program and compares it with other home care programs.

MENAKER, ELLA R. The extramural care of a modern home for the aged. *Geriatrics,* v. 20, November 1965: 983–988.

Home care program initiated and supervised by the Jewish Home and Hospital for Aged, using services and facilities of other community agencies.

NASH, DAVID T. Home care for the chronically institutionalized. *Geriatrics,* v. 21, February 1966: 215–220.

Suggests the need for a new program of foster homes for elderly people, utilizing already established home care facilities.

NATIONAL COUNCIL ON THE AGING. HEALTH COMMITTEE. Home-delivered meals for the ill, handicapped, and elderly. A report by the Committee on Guidelines for the Project. New York, 1965. 86p. (*American Journal of Public Health,* v. 55, May 1965: supplement)

Conclusions from the findings of a comprehensive survey of portable meals programs.

NATIONAL LEAGUE FOR NURSING. Report of conference on public health nursing care of the sick at home. New York, 1953. 57p.

Reviews principles on which community services are planned and provided; statistics of ill health; the development of medical care programs in the framework of home care.

OEO and PHS launch projects to train older people as home health aides. *Aging,* no. 143, September 1966: 3–5; 24.

Purposes and description of the program.

ROTH, MITCHELL E., *and others.* The value of coordinated and comprehensive home care. *American Journal of Public Health,* v. 57, October 1967: 1841–1847.

Interdisciplinary evaluation and treatment involving centralized administration is an effective means of approaching a high level of patient care.

U.S. BUREAU OF HEALTH MANPOWER. DIVISION OF NURSING. Services available for nursing care of the sick at home, January 1966. Washington, U.S. Govt. Print. Off., 1967. 74p. (Public Health Service publication no. 1265—revised 1967)

Information on all agencies in the U.S., Puerto Rico, the Virgin Islands and Guam that offer an organized program of nursing care for the sick at home.

U.S. PUBLIC HEALTH SERVICE. Portraits in community health; dental care for the chronically ill. Washington, U.S. Govt. Print. Off., 1967. 24p. (Public Health Service publication no. 1344–4)

————.Portraits in community health; rural home nursing care for long-term illness. Washington, U.S. Govt. Print. Off., 1965. 24p. (Public Health Service publication no. 1344–1)

U.S. PUBLIC HEALTH SERVICE. Portraits in community health. The Dexter Manor story: health services in housing for the elderly. Washington, U.S. Govt. Print. Off., 1966. 25p. (Public health service publication no. 1344–3)

Describes a program designed to investigate the effectiveness of preventive health services and home nursing care to residents of a public housing project for the elderly.

————. DIVISION OF MEDICAL CARE ADMINISTRATION. Planning for home health services; a summary of developments in home health care following the enactment of Medicare and Medicaid. Rev. Arlington, Va., 1967. 9p.

WALDMAN, H. BARRY, and MURRAY STEIN. A plan for total dental services for the chronically ill and aged. Cleveland, Highland View Hospital, Dept. of Dentistry, 1967. 89p.

Describes a home care and outpatient program.

WORKSHOP ON HOME CARE SERVICES. Proceedings. Chicago, American Hospital Association, 1960. 96p.

Conducted under the joint sponsorship of: American Hospital Association; American Medical Association; Blue Cross Commission; Blue Shield Medical Care Plans; U.S. Public Health Service.

Hospitals—Services and Care

AMERICAN HOSPITAL ASSOCIATION. The extended care unit in a general hospital; a guide to planning, organization, and management. Chicago, 1966. 52p.

————. Hospital accreditation references. Chicago, 1964. 211p.

Source of assistance for hospitals attempting to meet the accreditation requirements of the Joint Commission on Accreditation of Hospitals.

BOE, PAUL A. The role of the Lutheran hospital in care of the aged. *Lutheran Social Welfare Quarterly,* v. 4, March 1964: 31–39.

Suggests hospitals re-examine their function and resources in order to meet total needs of the aged in the community.

COOK, FRED J. The plot against the patient. Englewood Cliffs, N.J., Prentice-Hall, 1967. 373p.

Documented report of the conditions in hospitals, the power of the medical establishment, and the chaos of medical care.

GASPARD, NANCY J., and CARL E. HOPKINS. Determinants of use of ambulatory medical services by an aged population. *Inquiry,* v. 4, March 1967: 28–36.

Rate of use of a comprehensive outpatient clinic service available to residents of a retirement village.

GLASER, BARNEY G., and ANSELM L. STRAUSS. Awareness of dying. Chicago, Aldine, 1965. 305p.

Focuses on the interaction between hospital staffs and patients.

JOINT COMMISSION ON ACCREDITATION OF HOSPITALS. Accredited hospitals. Chicago.

State listing of hospitals complying in the main with the standards. Hospitals with less than 25 beds are not eligible for accreditation.

KAUFMAN, M. RALPH, ed. The psychiatric unit in a general hospital; its current and future role. New York, International Universities Press, 1965. 482p.

The geriatric group, by *Alvin I. Goldfarb,* p. 240–268.

LIEDERMAN, PAUL C., *and others.* Outpatient group therapy with geriatric patients. *Geriatrics,* v. 22, January 1967: 148–153.

Presents a program of group therapy which may postpone or prevent the need for hospital or nursing home confinement.

LINN, LOUIS, ed. Frontiers in general hospital psychiatry. New York, International Universities Press, 1961. 483p.

Chapter 13: "Six weeks in, six weeks out: a program for geriatric patients," by John DeLargy.

REICHEL, WILLIAM. Complications in the care of five hundred elderly hospitalized patients. *Journal of the American Geriatrics Society,* v. 13, November 1965: 973–981.

Describes adverse effects of hospitalization on the elderly patient.

ROYLE, CHARLES M., and AGNES W. BREWSTER. The impact of aged patients on hospital use and income. *Public Health Reports,* v. 81, June 1966: 488–496.

Results of a three-month study of all discharges from the Albany Medical Center.

SOLON, JERRY A. Patterns of medical care: sociocultural variations among a hospital's outpatients. *American Journal of Public Health,* v. 56, June 1966: 884–894.

"Illustrates how relating patients' patterns of care to their sociocultural characteristics can offer useful perspective to the providers and planners of services."

STRANTZ, IRMA H., and WINSTON R. MILLER. Ambulation of "ambulatory" handicapped patients. *Geriatrics,* v. 21, November 1966: 177–186.

Study illustrates need for organized systems to transport patients to adequate clinical facilities.

TAUBENHAUS, LEON J., and JOHN G. McCORMICK. Outpatient clinics and the elderly: a study of usage. *Hospitals,* v. 38, April 16, 1964. 46–48; 136.

Explains the backgrounds and life situations that motivated elderly residents of Brookline, Mass. to use outpatient clinics.

U.S. NATIONAL CENTER FOR HEALTH STATISTICS. Hospital utilization in the last year of life; development and test of a method of measuring the effect of omitting decedents from a survey of hospitalization. Washington, U.S. Govt. Print. Off., 1965. 30p. (Public health service publication no. 1000—series 2—no. 10)

U.S. PUBLIC HEALTH SERVICE. Portraits in community health; aging center in Sinai Hospital. Washington, U.S. Govt. Print. Off., 1965. 31p. (Public Health Service publication no. 1344-2)
    Describes program of comprehensive health care to medically indigent aged persons.

WALSH, MAURICE J., and JOYCE M. CORNING. Aging: the challenges in institutional care. *Hospital Progress,* v. 46, May 1965: 120-125.
    Concept of total care of the aging should be rooted in the point of view that debility and disease are not age oriented nor the inevitable characteristics of older people.

Medical and Dental Care Programs

AMERICAN PUBLIC HEALTH ASSOCIATION. PROGRAM AREA COMMITTEE ON MEDICAL CARE ADMINISTRATION. A guide to medical care administration. Vol. 1. Concepts and principles. New York, 1965. 106p.
    Outlines set of principles for medical care administration.

ANDERSON, ODIN W., ed. Medical care. *Journal of Health and Human Behavior,* v. 5, Summer and Fall 1964: entire issue.
    Includes articles on health services, prepaid health plans, diagnosis in therapeutic practice, care of the chronically ill, and community homemaker services.

BLANCHARD, BRADFORD M. Geriatric care in the public housing area. *Geriatrics,* v. 19, April 1964: 302-308.
    Study, conducted in a low-income housing project, to determine how much and what kind of medical care was needed.

BLOCK, IRVIN. How to get good medical care. New York, Public Affairs Committee, 1965. 27p. (Public Affairs pamphlet no. 368)
    Describes recent studies of the quality of medical care, recommendations of experts, and guidelines to best chances for high quality care.

COMMISSION ON THE DELIVERY OF PERSONAL HEALTH SERVICES. Comprehensive community health services for New York City. New York, 1967. 60p.
    Findings and recommendations.

CROSBY, EDWIN L. Improving the delivery of health care services. *Hospitals,* v. 41, September 1, 1967: 53-58.
    Discusses patterns of delivery of medical care and describes attempts that are being made to improve them.

DeGroot, Leslie J., comp. Medical care; social and organizational aspects. Springfield, Ill., Thomas, 1966. 538p.

> Review and analysis.

Epstein, Bernard D. Medical care program for the elderly in a housing project. *Public Health Reports,* v. 79, November 1964: 1005–1014.

> Detailed description of a project devised to demonstrate the cost feasibility and value of offering a wide range of out-of-hospital services to residents of a public housing project who were 62 years or older.

Freeman, Howard E., *and others.* Use of medical resources by Spancos: 1. Extent and sources of medical care in a very old population. *American Journal of Public Health,* v. 56, September 1966: 1530–1539.

> Use of health resources by a group of the very aged, veterans of the Spanish-American War.

Graber, Joe Bales. Findings and implications of a nationwide program review of resources available to meet the health needs of the aging and aged. *Gerontologist,* v. 6, December 1966: 191–200.

> Program and administrative information gathered in 20 states during a two-year period by the Gerontology Branch in the Division of Chronic Diseases of the U.S. Public Health Service.

———. A 1965 report of programs on aging. *American Journal of Public Health,* v. 56, March 1966: 480–491.

> Review of the programs and activities of the Bureau of State Services, U.S. Public Health Service, which are related to the health of the aging and the aged.

New York Academy of Medicine. Closing the gap in the availability of health services. *Bulletin of the New York Academy of Medicine,* second series, v. 41, December 1965: entire issue.

> Papers presented at the 1965 Health Conference of the New York Academy of Medicine.

Pritchard, John G. Benefits of consecutive patient care. *Geriatrics,* v. 19, November 1964: 839–844.

> Discusses the positive points of consecutive patient care and attempts to justify the demarcation of patients by arbitrary recovery levels.

Randall, Ollie A. Social needs parallel medical needs of elderly patients. *Hospitals,* v. 41, October 16, 1967: 63–66.

> Summarizes several social needs essential to a good prognosis and suggests ways the health care institution can fill these needs.

REYNOLDS, FRANK W., and PAUL C. BARSAM. Adult health; services for the chronically ill and aged. New York, Macmillan, 1967. 242p.

Part One. Components of an adult health program. Part Two. Supporting services. Part Three. Categorical chronic disease control programs. Part Four. Federal and state programs and financing of costs.

ROEMER, MILTON I. The responsibility of public health for medical care of the aged. *Public Health Reports,* v. 78, October 1963: 856–860.

Urges that health services in the United States be organized, coordinated, and administered by public health agencies.

ROUTH, THOMAS A. High-level health for the elderly. *Journal of the American Geriatrics Society,* v. 14, May 1966: 533–538.

Proposes a plan to facilitate care of geriatric patients.

SCOTT, W. RICHARD, *and others,* eds. Medical care: readings in the sociology of medical institutions. New York, Wiley, 1966. 595p.

Discusses two basic medical roles, healer and patient; followed by aspects of the therapeutic relationship, and concludes with a series of papers on hospitals and clinics and their relationship to the larger community.

SHANAS, ETHEL. Medical care among those 65 and over, reported illness and utilization of health services by the "sick" and the "well." New York, Health Information Foundation, 1960. 35p. (HIF research series 16)

SIGMOND, ROBERT M. Health planning. *Medical Care,* v. 5, May-June 1967: 117–128.

Some of the major obstacles in the way of improvements in health planning with recommendations for overcoming them.

SIMONS, JOHN H. Prepaid dentistry: a case study. Berkeley, Institute of Industrial Relations, University of California, 1967. 47p.

Directed specifically at the effect of prepayment on the utilization of dental services and on the improvement of dental health.

Symposium on research in long-term care. *Gerontologist,* v. 4, June 1964: Pt. II.

Part I. Perspectives on long-term illness. Part II. Methodology for studies of long-term care. Part III. Contemporary research in long-term care.

U.S. CONGRESS. HOUSE. COMMITTEE ON VETERANS' AFFAIRS. Impact of Medicare on Veterans' Administration medical system. Washington, U.S. Govt. Print. Off., 1966. 67p. (89th Cong., 2d sess., House committee print no. 177)

Results of a questionnaire sent to a group of 10,000 veterans on the pension rolls asking whether the veteran would elect to receive care in a VA hospital, in a community hospital under Medicare, or in a community hospital at his own expense.

U.S. CONGRESS. SENATE. SPECIAL COMMITTEE ON AGING. Needs for services revealed by Operation Medicare Alert; a report by the Subcommittee on Federal, State and Community Services. Washington, U.S. Govt. Print. Off., 1966. 15p. (89th Cong., 2d sess., committee print)

> Report on needs with recommendations of action needed.

U.S. DEPT. OF HEALTH, EDUCATION, AND WELFARE. OFFICE OF PROGRAM COORDINATION. To improve medical care; a guide to federal financial aid for the development of medical care; services, facilities, personnel. Rev. ed. Washington, U.S. Govt. Print. Off., 1966. 96p.

U.S. PUBLIC HEALTH SERVICE. Economic benefits from public health services; objectives, methods, and examples of measurement. Washington, U.S. Govt. Print. Off., 1964. 31p. (Public Health Service publication no. 1178)

> Report of a symposium which included discussions from the fields of dental health, mental health, nursing, and vocational rehabilitation.

————. What thirteen local health departments are doing in medical care. Washington, U.S. Govt. Print. Off., 1967. 128p. (Public Health Service publication no. 1664)

> Series of descriptive and analytical investigations of the medical care activities of 13 local departments.

Nursing Homes and Other Geriatric Facilities

ALFORD, ELISABETH M. A new era for the nursing home. *Journal of the South Carolina Medical Association,* v. 63, June 1967: 226–230.
> History and future growth of nursing homes.

AMERICAN NURSING HOME INSTITUTE. Financing nursing home care. Washington, American Nursing Home Association, 1961. 107p.

BAUMGARTEN, HAROLD, JR. Concepts of nursing home administration; a manual for executives of prolonged-illness institutions. New York, Macmillan, 1965. 370p.

BEATTIE, WALTER M., JR. Responsibility of the long-term facility to the long-term patient. *Hospitals,* v. 38, September 1, 1964: 65–69.
> Two-and-a-half-year study of facilities in the St. Louis area for caring for chronically ill and aged persons.

BINDER, GERTRUDE. Establishing and maintaining standards for long-term care institutions. *Hospitals,* v. 41, October 16, 1967: 80–87.
> Points to the need for clear definitions of the various types of long-term care institutions and observes that the regulatory agency will need to reassess the scope of its functions and also its approach to staffing.

Buerki, Robert A., ed. Pharmaceutical services for nursing homes. Proceedings of the conference held at the Ohio State University, September 7–10, 1965. Columbus, Ohio, Ohio State University, 1966. 131p.

Care of the nursing home patients with respect to pharmaceutical services as provided for by state laws and federal programs.

California Association of Nursing Homes, Sanitariums, Rest Homes and Homes for the Aged. Uniform accounting system for nursing and convalescent homes. Sacramento, 1966. 62p.

Catholic Hospital Association of the United States and Canada. The administration of long-term care facilities; nursing homes, homes for the aged, chronic and convalescent homes. St. Louis, 1960. 60p.

Adapted from speeches delivered at an institute held February 25–27, 1960, and is an initial effort on the part of the association in the field of the care of the aged.

Collins, Jerome A., and others. Is the nursing home the mental hospital's back ward in the community? *Journal of the American Geriatrics Society*, v. 15, January 1967: 75–81.

Compares the nursing home, and other facilities caring for long-term mental patients, with the back ward of the custodial mental hospitals of the past.

Daugherty, Jewel S., and others. Planning, developing and equipping a physical medicine and rehabilitation program in an extended care facility. *Professional Nursing Home*, v. 8, May 1966: 10–20.

Doff, S. D., and others. Orienting the architect to nursing home design. *Public Health Reports*, v. 80, December 1965: 1077–1082.

Describes several projects in Florida for educating the architect in designing nursing homes.

Evans, Roger, and Charles E. Lewis. Studies of adult care homes. *Journal of the Kansas Medical Society*, v. 46, June 1965: 282–289.

Part I. Attitudes of residents and relatives. Part II. Attitudes of employees and a prospective study of residents.

Follmann, J. F., Jr. Health insurance and nursing home care; a study. Rev. ed. Chicago, Health Insurance Association of America, 1963. 127p.

Survey of nursing homes, nursing home care, and scope of health insurance coverage.

Grant, E. J. Nursing home maintenance: a big job on a small budget. *Nursing Home Administrator*, v. 17, September–October 1963: 22–24; 51–54.

Suggestions for reducing maintenance costs without sacrificing cleanliness, safety precautions and quality.

HAMMOND, ROBERT P. New Ferncrest home in Seattle to place great emphasis on physiotherapy facilities. *Nursing Home Administrator,* v. 17, September-October 1963: 6–8; 34–36.

HOOPER, LANGDON, and PAUL A. McWILLIAMS, eds. Care of the nursing-home patient. Boston, Little, 1967. 235p.
Guide for those concerned with the total medical-care program for the elderly patient.

HUFFMAN, EDNA K. Medical records in nursing homes. Berwyn, Ill., Physicians' Record Co., 1961. 204p.
Includes material to help the nursing home meet licensing requirements in a state that is just setting up such standards.

JACOBS, H. LEE, and WOODROW W. MORRIS, eds. Nursing and retirement home administration. Ames, Iowa, Iowa State University Press, 1966. 301p.

JOINT COMMISSION ON ACCREDITATION OF HOSPITALS. Accredited extended care facilities. Chicago, 1966. 34p.
List divided according to classification: extended care facilities, intermediate care facilities, domiciliary facilities and mental facilities.

KAPLAN, HIRSH. A community nursing home. Washington, U.S. Govt. Print. Off., 1961. 16p. (Patterns for progress in aging, case study no. 1)
Study of the Phoenix Jewish Kivel Nursing Home.

————. Function and form. *Nursing Homes,* v. 12, November 1963: 14–15.
Nursing home administrator stresses need for special designs for nursing homes.

LEVEY, SAMUEL. Bringing the nursing home into the mainstream of medical care. *Hospitals,* v. 40, January 1, 1966: 56–60.
Outlines some of the problems of properly integrating the nursing home industry with other medical care institutions.

LINN, MARGARET W. A nursing home rating scale. *Geriatrics,* v. 21, October 1966: 188–200.
Suggested rating scale as a means of determining which nursing homes are more likely to provide good care.

McQUILLAN, FLORENCE L. Fundamentals of nursing home administration. Philadelphia, Saunders, 1967. 395p.
Highlights the needs of today's nursing home facilities and the setting of this specific facility in the total health care field.

Marian Hall foods department manual. *Professional Nursing Home,* v. 6, March 1964: 33–44.

Manual of a 150-bed home in Flint, Michigan. Functions and policies for all employees of the foods department.

Marian Hall nursing department manual. *Professional Nursing Home,* v. 7, April 1965: 39–66.

Manual of a 150-bed home in Flint, Michigan. Describes functions and policies for nurses, nurse's aides and food service employees.

MILLER, MICHAEL B. The nursing home, society, and the law. *Geriatrics,* v. 21, March 1966: 193–198.

Nursing homes should be nonsurgical chronic disease hospitals, with psychiatric orientation, to provide proper rehabilitation care.

NATIONAL CONFERENCE ON NURSING HOMES AND HOMES FOR THE AGED, Washington, D.C., 1958. Report. Washington, U.S. Govt. Print. Off., 1958. 85p. (Public Health Service publication no. 625)

Principal addresses, background information, recommendations, and discussions which led to the development of the recommendations.

NATIONAL NURSING HOME INSTITUTE. Improving patient care through education and regulation. Proceedings. Washington, American Nursing Home Association, n.d. 109p.

Institute conducted by the American Nursing Home Association in cooperation with the U.S. Public Health Service, October 12–14, 1960.

NATIONAL SAFETY COUNCIL. Safety manual for nursing homes and homes for the aged. Washington, American Nursing Home Association, 1962. 51p.

NATIONAL SOCIAL WELFARE ASSEMBLY. NATIONAL COMMITTEE ON THE AGING. Standards of care for older people in institutions. New York, 1953. 3v.

Contents: I. Suggested standards for homes for the aged and nursing homes. II. Methods of establishing and maintaining standards in homes for the aged and nursing homes. III. Bridging the gap between existing practices and desirable goals in homes for the aged and nursing homes.

NICHOLSON, EDNA E. Planning new institutional facilities for long-term care. New York, Putnam, 1956. 358p.

Discusses need for facilities, the organization and program of a new unit, the building and equipment, and the costs.

PENCHANSKY, ROY, and LEON J. TAUBENHAUS. Institutional factors affecting the quality of care in nursing homes. *Geriatrics,* v. 20, July 1965: 591–598.

Improvement of patient care depends on solving problems posed by small bed capacity, method of reimbursement for welfare patients, and requirements of different levels of care.

PREHEIM, D. V. Accreditation of nursing homes. *Journal of the Kansas Medical Society,* v. 46, June 1965: 290–292.

Explains NCANH program for nursing home accreditation.

RANDALL, OLLIE A. The situation with nursing homes. *American Journal of Nursing,* v. 65, November 1965: 92–97.

Reports that too many nursing homes are considered a business first, a service second.

RHETTS, JOHN E., and BERNARD A. STOTSKY. The nursing home: therapeutic community or little state hospital for psychiatric patients? *Journal of the American Geriatrics Society,* v. 13, November 1965: 982–988.

Discusses differences in attitudes of the researchers and the nursing home toward patients, with case illustrations.

SAMIS, SIDNEY M., and LOUIS HALPRYN. A television-based training program for nurse's aides in nursing homes. *Public Health Reports,* v. 80, August 1965: 731–736.

Description of the New York City Department of Hospitals' training program to improve the quality of nursing care given to patients in the city's proprietary nursing homes.

SHAFFER, HELEN B. Nursing homes and medical care. *Editorial Research Reports,* 1963, v. 2, No. 17, Nov. 6, 1963: entire issue.

SMIGEL, JOSEPH O., *and others.* Nursing home administration. Springfield, Ill., Thomas, 1962. 227p.

Written for owners, administrators and supervisors in nursing institutions or hospital supervision.

SOLON, JERRY ALAN. Medical care: its social and organizational aspects; nursing homes and medical care. *New England Journal of Medicine,* v. 269, November 14, 1963: 1067–1074.

Examines the organizational character of the nursing home, the type of patient found there, its staffing pattern, and its relation with physicians and hospitals.

STOTSKY, BERNARD. The psychiatric patient in the nursing home: a retrospective study. *Journal of the American Geriatrics Society,* v. 14, July 1966: 735–747.

Study to determine whether factors relating to the patient or factors relating to the physical or social milieu were more significant for the known outcome of placement in nursing homes of 141 patients from state mental hospitals.

TAUBENHAUS, LEON J. The nursing home as a facility for the management of the chronically ill. *Journal of the American Geriatrics Society,* v. 13, June 1965: 509–514.

Discusses the role of the nursing home and its organization and structure.

TERMAN, LOUIS A. Selecting a "home" for the elderly and chronically ill: the physician's role. *Geriatrics,* v. 20, July 1965: 599–604.

Describes various types of nursing homes in order to assist the physician in finding the proper home for his patient.

U.S. BUREAU OF LABOR STATISTICS. Industry wage survey; nursing homes and related facilities, April 1965. Washington, U.S. Govt. Print. Off., 1966. 72p. (Bulletin no. 1492.)

Survey of employee earnings and supplementary benefits in nursing homes and related facilities in April 1965.

U.S. CONGRESS. SENATE. COMMITTEE ON LABOR AND PUBLIC WELFARE. Nursing home care for veterans. Washington, U.S. Govt. Print. Off., 1964. 66p. (88th Cong., 2d sess., rept. no. 1293.)

U.S. DEPT. OF HOUSING AND URBAN DEVELOPMENT. Study of FHA assisted nursing homes. Washington, 1966. 32p.

Study of the characteristics of 185 homes which had received final endorsement for FHA insurance.

————. Minimum property standards for nursing homes. Washington, U.S. Govt. Print. Off., 1967. 68p.

Standards adopted to provide a basis of acceptability for the physical security for insured mortgages on nursing home properties.

U.S. NATIONAL CENTER FOR HEALTH STATISTICS. Characteristics of residents in institutions for the aged and chronically ill, United States— April-June 1963. Washington, U.S. Govt. Print. Off., 1965. 53p. (Public Health Service publication no. 1000—series 12—no. 2.)

Statistics on age, sex, color, length of stay, and selected health characteristics.

————.Employees in nursing and personal care homes: number, work experience, special training, and wages, United States, May–June 1964. Washington, U.S. Govt. Print. Off., 1967. (Public Health Service publication no. 1000—series 12—no. 6.)

Statistics on the number and types of employees and their total work experience in nursing and personal care homes and hospitals.

————. Employees in nursing and personal care homes, United States, May-June 1964. Washington, U.S. Govt. Print. Off., 1966. 34p. (Public Health Service publication no. 1000, series 12, no. 5.)

Age and sex of employees, job categories, hours worked, and ratio of residents to employees.

————. Utilization of institutions for the aged and chronically ill, United States, April-June 1963. Washington, U.S. Govt. Print. Off., 1966. 35p. (Public Health Service publication no. 1000—series 12— no. 4.)

Number of beds, admissions, discharges, recipients of public assistance, and rate of occupancy.

U.S. Public Health Service. How to organize a health record system; a guide for nursing homes and homes for the aged. Washington, U.S. Govt. Print. Off., 1966. 54p. (Public Health Service publication no. 1429.)

Joint publication of the American Association of Medical Record Librarians and the Public Health Service.

————. Nursing home standard guide; recommendations relating to standards for establishing, maintaining, and operating nursing homes. Washington, U.S. Govt. Print. Off., 1961. 63p. (Public Health Service publication no. 827.)

————. Nursing homes and related facilities factbook. Washington, U.S. Govt. Print. Off., 1963. 177p. (Public Health Service publication no. 930–F–4.)

Highlight data includes statistics on facilities available, cost per day, monthly charges, financial support, public assistance payments, and homemaker services

————. Nursing homes: environmental health factors. Vol. I. Introduction. Washington, U.S. Govt. Print. Off., 1963. 16p. (Public Health Service publication no. 1009–1.)

Describes the nursing home resident and his environment, and documents the increasing need for nursing homes.

————. Division of Hospital and Medical Facilities. A suggested system of uniform expense accounting for nursing homes and related fields. Washington, U.S. Govt. Print. Off., 1961. 125p. (Public Health Service publication no 835.)

U.S. Welfare Administration. Open every door; the goal for nursing homes and Title VI of the Civil Rights Act of 1964. Washington, U.S. Govt. Print. Off., 1967. 14p.

Examples of the process of integrating formerly segregated nursing homes.

Vanston, A. Rorke, and others. A comparative study of 40 nursing homes; their design and use. Washington, U.S. Govt. Print. Off., 1965. 26p (Public Health Service publication no. 930–D–17.)

Summary of the findings of a survey of the characteristics of nursing homes, including general operating features, nonclinical characteristics of the patients, architectural design, construction and cost data, and evaluation of the physical facilities in relation to the care provided.

Waldman, H. Barry. The problems of nursing home dental care. *Journal of the American Dental Association,* v. 74, February 1967: 423–425.

Describes a program in which 120 general practitioners and specialists and 65 nursing homes participated.

WILLIAMS, RALPH C., *and others.* Nursing home management. New York, Dodge, 1959. 230p.

Intended to serve as a reference for persons of varying backgrounds who need information relating to the general field of nursing home management.

WOLK, ROBERT L., and ROCHELLE B. SEIDEN. A contagious disease: old age. *Journal of the American Geriatrics Society,* v. 13, April 1965: 343–347.

Explores the question as to whether homes for the aged, job placement offices for older people, and other facilities devoted exclusively to aged people, hasten or deter the aging process.

ZAMPELLA, A. D. Accreditation and the adjuvant effects on convalescent home operation. *Journal of the American Geriatrics Society,* v. 12, July 1964: 658–664.

Beneficial effects of accreditation upon the day-to-day operation of a nursing home.

ZUCHOVITZ, SADIE. Selected characteristics of proprietary nursing homes in New York State and their patients, 1965. Albany, New York State Dept. of Health, 1967. 8p. (Health economic reports 67–3.)

Summary of findings and tables.

Nursing Services

ABDELLAH, FAYE G., *and others.* Patient-centered approaches to nursing. New York, Macmillan, 1960. 205p.

"Purpose of this book is to provide a basis upon which patient-centered approaches to nursing can be utilized by the nurse educator, the nurse practitioner, and the hospital administrator."

ADAMS, G. F., and P. L. McILWRAITH. Geriatric nursing; a study of the work of geriatric ward staff. London, Oxford University Press, 1963. 77p.

Comparison of nursing activities in geriatric and general medical wards.

The aged in our society. *Nursing Outlook,* v. 12, November 1964: entire issue.

Articles concerned with how nurses can help older persons at home, in the hospital, and in the nursing home.

BENFER, BEVERLY A. Adding years to life. *Nursing Homes,* v. 13, September 1964: 12–14.

Problems involved in geriatric-psychiatric nursing and the great potential for the future.

BLUMBERG, JEANNE E., and ELEANOR E. DRUMMOND. Nursing care of the long-term patient. New York, Springer, 1963. 134p.

Attitudes toward the long-term patient and his family.

BUCKLEY, BONITA RICE. Nursing care of the aged. Madison, University of Wisconsin, 1962. 36p.

Concerned with special nursing problems of some aged patients.

CATHOLIC UNIVERSITY OF AMERICA. WORKSHOP ON CONTINUITY OF PATIENT CARE: THE ROLE OF NURSING. Continuity of patient care: the role of nursing. Proceedings . . . Washington, 1966. 232p.

Covers the components of the continuity of patient care as they relate to the responsibilities of nurse practitioners, educators and administrators in the various health related institutions in the country.

Challenges to nursing in Medicare. *American Journal of Nursing*, v. 65, November 1965: 68–75.

Seven nursing experts discuss opportunities for improving patient care under the new health insurance program.

COMMUNITY SERVICE SOCIETY OF NEW YORK. COMMITTEE ON HEALTH. Continuity in care for impaired older persons; public health nursing in a geriatric rehabilitation maintenance program. New York, 1964. 172p.

Statistical measurement of the effectiveness of a public health nursing program on a group of disabled persons over 60 years of age who had completed a hospital program of rehabilitation training and had been discharged.

———. ———. Service following rehabilitation training; a description of public health nursing service offered a group of disabled older persons. New York, 1965. 82p.

Describes the problems confronting patients and the service given by public health nurses.

EXTON-SMITH, A. N. An investigation of geriatric nursing problems in hospital. London, National Corporation for the Care of Old People, 1962. 238p.

Study of the basic nursing care of old people in hospitals.

HODKINSON, MARY A. Nursing the elderly. New York, Pergamon Press, 1966. 154p.

General nursing procedures and problems, as well as nursing of specific disorders.

HULICKA, IRENE M. Fostering self-respect in aged patients. *American Journal of Nursing*, v. 64, March 1964: 84–89.

Shows how in small ways nurses can compensate patients for what they lack.

INGBAR, MARY LEE, *and others*. Differences in the costs of nursing services: a statistical study of community hospitals in Massachusetts. *American Journal of Public Health*, v. 56, October 1966: 1699–1715.

JAEGER, PHILIP. Better nursing care for the indigent aged. *Journal of the American Geriatrics Society,* v. 11, August 1963: 797–800.
Recommendations for the improvement of paramedical and nursing care of the indigent elderly.

JOHNSTON, DOROTHY F. Total patient care; foundations and practice. St. Louis, Mosby, 1964. 550p.
Chapter 8. Nursing the geriatric patient.

KOOS, EARL LOMON. The sociology of the patient. New York, McGraw-Hill, 1959. 266p.
Textbook to help the student nurse to understand something of why man behaves as he does and how all this relates to his health or illness.

KOZIER, BARBARA BLACKWOOD, and BEVERLY WITTER DuGAS. Fundamentals of patient care; a comprehensive approach to nursing. Philadelphia, Saunders, 1967. 386p.

MILLER, MICHAEL B. The physiological basis of nursing problems of the chronically ill aged. *Journal of the American Geriatrics Society,* v. 14, March 1966: 244–257.
Study shows primary cause of disability in the chronically ill aged is arterial disease of the brain and need for psycho-social nursing techniques.

MORISSEY, ALICE B. Rehabilitation nursing. New York, Putnam, 1951. 299p.
Function and practice of nursing in rehabilitation.

NATIONAL HEALTH COUNCIL. COMMITTEE ON RESEARCH. Research in patient care (with special emphasis on comprehensive care of the chronically ill and aging). New York, 1960. Various paging.
Report of a meeting held January 19, 1960. Includes papers by: *Faye G. Abdellah, Doris Schwartz,* and *Harold M. Willard.*

NATIONAL LEAGUE FOR NURSING. Continuity of nursing care from hospital to home; a study in a voluntary general hospital. New York, 1966. 241p.
The ways hospitals and out-of-hospital nursing services can work together to assure continuing patient care.

————. Report of a work conference on nursing in long-term chronic disease and aging. New York, 1960. 43p.

————. DEPARTMENT OF PUBLIC HEALTH NURSING. How to organize and extend community nursing services for the care of the sick at home. New York, 1962. 96p.

NEWTON, KATHLEEN. Geriatric nursing. 3rd ed. St. Louis, Mosby, 1960. 483p.

> Considers in detail the more common clinical conditions that need emphasis. New chapters added in this edition briefly survey the care of the aged and chronically ill in the general hospital, mental hospital, their own homes, nursing homes, and elsewhere.

SCHWARTZ, DORIS, and others. The elderly ambulatory patient: nursing and psychosocial needs. New York, Macmillan, 1964. 356p.

> Long-term research project conducted at New York-Cornell University Medical Center.

SHANKS, MARY D., and DOROTHY A. KENNEDY. The theory and practice of nursing service administration. New York, McGraw-Hill, 1965. 303p.

> Defines the kind of person needed to do the job, the kind of place where much of the job is done, and the process through which the job is successfully accomplished.

SHAPIRO, SAM, and MARILYN M. EINHORN. Changes in rates of visiting nurse services in the Health Insurance Plan. *American Journal of Public Health*, v. 54, March 1964: 417–430.

> Analysis of the utilization of visiting nurse services by members of the Health Insurance Plan of Greater New York during 1955–1960.

SMITH, EMILY M. Nursing services for the aged in housing projects and day centers. *American Journal of Nursing*, v. 65, December 1965: 72–74.

> Describes out-of-hospital based programs designed to help the well aged to remain healthy.

STEVENS, MARION KEITH. Geriatric nursing for practical nurses. Philadelphia, Saunders, 1965. 271p.

> The older patient, his special needs and problems, and some of the ways in which caring for this patient differs from nursing the general medical-surgical patient.

STEWART, WILLIAM H., and VIRGINIA V. VAHEY. Nursing services to the sick at home in selected communities. *American Journal of Public Health*, v. 54, March 1964: 407–416.

> Indicates need for broader and more comprehensive evaluation of current and future role of nursing services for care in the home.

TESTOFF, ARTHUR, and EUGENE LEVINE. Nursing care supplied to older people in their homes. *American Journal of Public Health*, v. 55, April 1965: 541–547.

> Study to determine how much nursing service was provided by public health agencies to older people in their homes.

U.S. NATIONAL CENTER FOR HEALTH STATISTICS. Institutions for the aged and chronically ill, United States, April-June 1963. Washington, U.S. Govt. Print. Off., 1965. 46p. (Public Health Service publication no. 1000, series 12, no. 1.)

Statistics on number and types of institutions for the aged according to nursing service provided, type of nurse in charge of nursing care, admission policies, and charges for care.

VISITING NURSE SERVICE OF NEW YORK. Public health nursing for the sick at home; a descriptive study. New York, 1967. 228p.

Primarily concerned with voluntary agency visiting nurses.

ZEMAN, FREDERIC D. Guidelines for the professional nurse in geriatric drug therapy. *Hospitals,* v. 41, March 1, 1967; 67; 70–73.

Emphasizes the importance of the professional nurse's function in the practical management of drug therapy.

Nutrition

AMERICAN HOSPITAL ASSOCIATION. Diet and menu guide. Chicago, 1961. 36p.

A project of the joint committee of the American Hospital Association and the American Dietetic Association.

BOGERT, L. JEAN, *and others.* Nutrition and physical fitness. 8th ed. Philadelphia, Saunders, 1966. 614p.

Chapter 23. Nutrition of older persons, pp. 440–451.

DIBBLE, M. V., *and others.* Evaluation of the nutritional status of elderly subjects, with a comparison between fall and spring. *Journal of the American Geriatrics Society,* v. 15, November 1967: 1031–1061.

Separate surveys conducted during fall and spring of 214 volunteers over the age of 50 living in public housing.

EAGLES, JUANITA A., ed. Aging and the nutritional problems of the aged. Harrisburg, Pa. Department of Health, 1960. 53p.

Second Public Health Nutrition Institute, sponsored by the University of Pittsburgh, the Commonwealth of Pennsylvania Department of Health, and the Allegheny County Health Department.

GALDSTON, IAGO, ed. Human nutrition; historic and scientific. New York, International Universities Press, 1960. 321p. (New York Academy of Medicine. Institute of Social and Historical Medicine, monograph III.)

GASTON, ALICE. Acceptability of portable cooking appliances by the elderly. *Journal of Home Economics,* v. 58, May 1966: 376–380.

Factors which might influence acceptability by the elderly of substituting a set of portable electric cooking appliances for a standard apartment-size range.

GOODHART, ROBERT S., and MICHAEL G. WOHL. Manual of clinical nutrition. Philadelphia, Lea, 1964. 279p.

Guide to good nutrition in brief, outline form.

GORDON, BEULAH M. A feeding plan for geriatric patients. *Hospitals,* v. 39, April 16, 1965: 92–98.

Describes a food service system at a long-term hospital in California.

GUGGENHEIM, K., and I. MARGULIC. Factors in the nutrition of elderly people living alone or as couples and receiving community assistance. *Journal of the American Geriatrics Society,* v. 12, June 1965: 561–568.

Food consumption and nutritional status of a group of elderly people subsisting mainly by public assistance.

HARRIS, CATHERINE F. Handbook of dietetics for nurses. 2nd ed. London, Baillier, 1963. 232p.

First part deals with normal nutrition. Second part is devoted to diet therapy in specific diseases.

HOWE, PHYLLIS S. Nutrition for practical nurses. 4th ed. Philadelphia, Saunders, 1967. 302p.

Normal nutrition, diet therapy, and the selection and care of food.

INSTITUTE ON NUTRITION IN CHRONIC DISEASE AND IN RELATION TO AGING AND CARE OF THE AGED. Report. Chapel Hill, University of North Carolina, School of Public Health, 1962. 219p.

Sponsored by the North Carolina State Board of Health; the School of Public Health, University of North Carolina; and the Division of Chronic Diseases, Public Health Service, U.S. Department of Health, Education, and Welfare.

JOHNS HOPKINS UNIVERSITY. SCHOOL OF HYGIENE AND PUBLIC HEALTH. Symposium on problems of gerontology; proceedings of a symposium held under the auspices of the Johns Hopkins University, School of Hygiene and Public Health and the National Vitamin Foundation. New York, National Vitamin Foundation, 1954. 141p.

KING, CHARLES GLEN, and GEORGE BRITT. Food hints for mature people; more years to life—more life to years. New York, Public Affairs Committee, 1962. 28p. (Public Affairs pamphlet no. 336.)

Prepared in cooperation with the Nutrition Foundation.

KRAUSE, MARIE V. Food, nutrition and diet therapy. 4th ed. Philadelphia, Saunders, 1966. 687p.

Chapter 15. Geriatric nutrition.

LEBOVIT, CORINNE. The food of older persons living at home. *Journal of the American Dietetic Association,* v. 46, April 1965: 285–289.

Survey of food consumption conducted of older households in Rochester, N.Y., in the spring of 1957.

LeBovit, Corinne, and Dorothy A. Baker. Food consumption and dietary levels of older households in Rochester, N.Y. Washington, U.S. Dept. of Agriculture, 1965. 91p. (Home economics research report no. 25.)

Study of OASDI beneficiaries that shows the influence of such characteristics as income, age, health, and marital status on food consumption.

MacDonald, Phyllis. A cookbook for the leisure years; with dividends for you of money, time and energy. Garden City, N.Y., Doubleday, 1967. 202p.

Guide to nutritious, easy to prepare, moderately priced meals.

———. The golden age cookbook. Garden City, N.Y., Doubleday, 1961. 192p.

Menus, recipes, party dishes, and diet.

McHenry, E. W. Basic nutrition. Philadelphia, Lippincott, 1957. 389p.

Written for use by students in colleges, universities, and schools of nursing.

National Research Council. Food and Nutrition Board. Recommended dietary allowances. Rev. Washington, 1958. 36p. (Publication 589.)

Allowances are for healthy, moderately active persons. Represent quantities actually consumed and do not allow for losses due to storage, cooking, or serving.

———. ———. The role of dietary fat in human health; a report of the Food and Nutrition Board. Washington, 1958. 32p. (Publication 575.)

Considers whether changes in kind or quantity of food fat would be beneficial to health.

Nutritionists, dietitians, and Medicare. *Journal of the American Dietetic Association,* v. 50, January 1967: 17.

Series of articles include: an overview of Medicare; the dietary department in hospitals; dietary services in extended care facilities; nutrition services in home health agencies.

Peyton, Alice B. Practical nutrition, 2d ed. Philadelphia, Lippincott, 1962. 434p.

Revision explains normal nutrition, diet therapy, and food economics.

Piper, Geraldine M., and Emily M. Smith. Geriatric nutrition. *Nursing Outlook,* v. 12, November 1964: 51–53.

Considers some of the factors that may be obstacles to adequate nutrition.

Riccitelli, M. L. Importance of therapeutic nutrition in the aged and infirm. *Journal of the American Geriatrics Society,* v. 12, May 1964: 489–492.

Benefits of nutrition in the intensive treatment of illness in the aged.

SHERMAN, HENRY C., and CAROLINE SHERMAN LANFORD. Essentials of nutrition. 4th ed. New York, Macmillan, 1957.

Approach is through the relation of food to health and efficiency.

STEINKAMP, RUTH C., *and others*. Re-survey of an aging population—fourteen-year follow-up. The San Mateo nutrition study. *Journal of the American Dietetic Association,* v. 46, February, 1965: 103–110.

A population group under study since 1948 regarding nutritional status, dietary habits, morbidity experience, and mortality.

SWANSON, PEARL. Adequacy in old age. Part I: role of nutrition. Part II: nutrition education programs for the aging. *Journal of Home Economics,* v. 56, November 1964: 651–658; December 1964: 728–734.

TURNER, DOROTHEA. Handbook of diet therapy. 4th ed. Chicago, University of Chicago Press, 1965. 260p.

Names, defines, and describes therapeutic diets in terms of current dietetic principles.

U.S. AGRICULTURAL RESEARCH SERVICE. Food guide for older folks. Washington, U.S. Govt. Print. Off.

Frequent revisions.

U.S. PUBLIC HEALTH SERVICE. A guide to nutrition and food service for nursing homes and homes for the aged. Washington, U.S. Govt. Print. Off., 1965. 87p. (Public Health Service publication no. 1309.)

Practical guidance on details of food service, in addition to explaining the principles of nutrition.

WATKIN, DONALD M. New findings in nutrition of older people. *American Journal of Public Health,* v. 55, April 1965: 548–553.

Ways of carrying out health workers' obligation to make better use of knowledge and techniques to promote preventive nutrition in youth and middle age.

WILSON, EVA D., *and others*. Principles of nutrition. 2nd ed. New York, Wiley, 1965. 596p.

Nutrition during aging, pp. 470–477.

WOHL, MICHAEL G., and ROBERT S. GOODHART, eds. Modern nutrition in health and disease. 3rd ed. Philadelphia, Lea, 1965. 1282p.

Application of nutrition to the everyday problems of public health and clinical medicine.

Rehabilitation

AMERICAN PUBLIC HEALTH ASSOCIATION. TECHNICAL DEVELOPMENT BOARD. PROGRAM AREA COMMITTEE ON CHRONIC DISEASE AND REHABILITATION. Chronic disease and rehabilitation; a program guide for state and local health agencies. New York, 1960. 116p.

BERNSTEIN, LEON. Economics and geriatric rehabilitation. *Geriatrics,* v. 21, July 1966: 199–204.

Discusses society's attitudes toward rehabilitation of the elderly in terms of humanitarian and economic considerations.

————. Variable patterns of rehabilitation care. *Geriatrics,* v. 21, February 1966: 189–193.

The differential role of the physician in three rehabilitation cases.

BLACK, BERTRAM J. The workshop in a changing world; the three faces of the sheltered workshop. *Rehabilitation Literature,* v. 26, August 1965: 230–235; 243.

Development, problems, and directions from three viewpoints: social-psychological, public health, and composite.

CHAFEE, CHARLES E. Rehabilitation needs of nursing home patients; a report of a survey. *Rehabilitation Literature,* v. 28, December 1967: 377–378; 382.

CONFERENCE ON REHABILITATION OF THE OLDER DISABLED WORKER. Proceedings. Institute, W. Va., 1964. 37p.

Sponsored by the West Virginia Vocational Rehabilitation Division in cooperation with the U.S. Vocational Rehabilitation Administration.

CONFERENCE ON THE REHABILITATION OF THE OLDER DISABLED WORKER. THE ACADEMICIAN'S RESPONSIBILITY. Report of the proceedings. Washington, U.S. Vocational Rehabilitation Administration, 1965. 66p.

Main focus on the involvement of the academician in tackling the problem of the older disabled worker, as the trainer of the leader of tomorrow.

CONLEY, RONALD W. The economics of vocational rehabilitation. Baltimore, Johns Hopkins Press, 1965. 177p.

Focuses on the need for the federal-state vocational rehabilitation program and on its results.

DAVIS, W. CLAYTON, *and others.* Rehabilitation of the geriatric amputee: a plea for moderation. *Archives of Physical Medicine and Rehabilitation,* v. 48, January 1967: 31–36.

Experience indicates that the geriatric patient should be selected cautiously for prosthetic rehabilitation.

DONAHUE, WILMA T., *and others,* eds. Rehabilitation of the older worker. Ann Arbor, University of Michigan Press, 1953. 200p.

Papers from the fourth annual Conference on Aging held at the University of Michigan.

FEDERATION EMPLOYMENT AND GUIDANCE SERVICE. The vocational rehabilitation of older handicapped workers; demonstration of feasibility of vocational rehabilitation for vocationally handicapped persons 60 years of age and over. Final report. New York, 1963. 49p.

FONG, THEODORE C. C., and CHARLES G. BRIGGLE. Intensive rehabilitation of the aged. *Hospital and Community Psychiatry*, v. 18, January 1967: 27–28.

Brief description of a remotivation program for geriatric patients at a state mental hospital.

GOTTESMAN, LEONARD E. Resocialization of the geriatric mental patient. *American Journal of Public Health*, v. 55, December 1965: 1964–1970.

Study of a project to resocialize geriatric mental patients through milieu therapy.

GRAY, ROBERT M., *and others*. Social factors influencing the decision of severely disabled older persons to participate in a rehabilitation program. *Rehabilitation Literature*, v. 25, June 1964: 162–167; 177.

Based on observation that successful rehabilitation depends partially on availability of a social structure that will motivate patients to give up sick role.

HANF, LISELOTTE C., and JOHN B. O'CONNOR. A follow-up survey of predominantly older amputees. *Geriatrics*, v. 21, July 1966: 166–172.

Study shows that patients get more benefit if they sincerely want the prostheses to work.

HIRSCHBERG, GERALD G., *and others*. Rehabilitation; a manual for the care of the disabled and elderly. Philadelphia, Lippincott, 1964. 377p.

Concerned with specific disabilities, and with methods and procedures tested by the authors and proved to be effective, economical and practical.

HOMBURGER, FREDDY, and CHARLES D. BONNER. Medical care and rehabilitation of the aged and chronically ill. 2nd ed. Boston, Little, 1964. 321p.

Part one discusses therapeutic procedures especially applicable to aged patients or those with chronic forms of the disorders covered. Part two describes the roles of the various members of the professional team as well as that of the family.

KELMAN, HOWARD R., *and others*. Community status of discharged rehabilitation patients: results of a longitudinal study. *Archives of Physical Medicine and Rehabilitation*, v. 47, October 1966: 670–675.

Concerned with reasons for the success or failure of discharged chronically ill and disabled patients to thrive in the community following intensive hospital rehabilitation care.

KOBRYNSKI, B. Rehabilitation of the elderly patient. *Journal of the American Geriatrics Society*, v. 14, April 1966: 400–406.

Discusses the objectives of geriatric rehabilitation.

114

LAWTON, EDITH BUCHWALD. Activities of daily living for physical rehabilitation. New York, Blakiston, 1963. 301p.

Concentrates on techniques for training a handicapped patient to perform by himself the maximum daily activities at home, in his work, and in his social life.

LITMAN, THEODOR J. Influence of age on physical rehabilitation. *Geriatrics,* v. 19, March 1964: 202–207.

An intensive study of 100 patients undergoing physical rehabilitation showed little evidence that the patient's age alone is directly related to therapeutic performance.

LUCHTERHAND, ELMER, and DANIEL SYDIAHA. Choice in human affairs; an application to aging-accident-illness problems. New Haven, Conn., College and University Press, 1966. 176p.

Describes a project for placing blue-collar workers who have experienced partial loss of physical capacity due to aging, accidents or illness.

MARTIN, LILLIEN JANE, and CLARE DeGRUCHY. Salvaging old age. New York, Macmillan, 1930. 175p.

Experiences of a consulting psychologist and her assistant in rehabilitating elderly people.

MILLER, MICHAEL B. Physical, emotional and social rehabilitation in a nursing-home population. *Journal of the American Geriatrics Society,* v. 13, February 1965: 176–185.

Describes daily level of functioning among patients in a semi-urban proprietary nursing home, the techniques used and the results obtained in a rehabilitation program involving 90 patients during a six-month period.

————. Synthesis of a therapeutic community for the aged ill. *Geriatrics,* v. 21, August 1966: 151–163.

Directed to the synthesis of milieu therapy for the chronically ill aged currently housed in a nursing home environment.

MURPHY, GEORGE E., and JOSEPH OGURA. Rehabilitation following laryngectomy. *Geriatrics,* v. 22, December 1967: 119–125.

Rehabilitation program includes management of fear, physical appearance, family reaction, and depression.

NATIONAL ASSOCIATION OF SHELTERED WORKSHOPS AND HOMEBOUND PROGRAMS. A guide to comprehensive rehabilitation services to the homebound disabled. Washington, U.S. Office of Vocational Rehabilitation, 1961. 136p.

Identification of services to the homebound for the state or community wishing to consider such a program.

NATIONAL REHABILITATION ASSOCIATION. COMMITTEE ON AGING. Rehabilitation for the aging; a growing responsibility. A statement of position on the problems and needs of the aging as they relate to rehabilitation services and programs. Washington, 1960. n.p.

NATIONAL RESEARCH COUNCIL. COMMITTEE ON PROSTHETICS RESEARCH AND DEVELOPMENT. The geriatric amputee. Washington, 1961. 245p. (Publication 919.)

> Report of a conference held April 13-14, 1961. Topics included surgical, medical, and prosthetic management of the aging amputee and the energy, biomechanical, sensory, neuromuscular, and psychosocial factors in their rehabilitation.

REED, JULIAN W., and JOHN COLLINS HARVEY. Rehabilitating the chronically ill; a method for evaluating the functional capacity of ambulatory patients. *Geriatrics,* v. 19, February 1964: 87-103.

Rehabilitating the aging disabled workers. *Rehabilitation Record,* v. 4, September-October 1963: 3-14.

> Five articles telling how oldsters in different parts of the country are being helped to achieve more satisfactory, productive lives.

ROTH, JULIUS A., and ELIZABETH M. EDDY. Rehabilitation for the unwanted. New York, Atherton Press, 1967. 232p.

> Report on the effectiveness of existing rehabilitation projects in a large-scale rehabilitation hospital.

RUSALEM, HERBERT. Penetrating the narrowing circle; a review of the literature concerning the vocational rehabilitation of homebound persons. *Rehabilitation literature,* v. 28, July 1967: 202-217.

> Surveys the literature that reflects previous experience in service to homebound persons with recommendations for future research.

——, *and others.* The vocational rehabilitation of older handicapped workers; demonstration of feasibility of vocational rehabilitation for vocationally handicapped persons 60 years of age and over. New York, Federation Employment and Guidance Service, 1963. 49p.

> The demonstration lasted 4 years and 2 months, November 1, 1957 to December 31, 1961.

RUSK, HOWARD A., *and others.* Rehabilitation medicine. St. Louis, Mosby, 1958. 572p.

> Chapter 27 deals with geriatric rehabilitation.

SHERMAN, E. DAVID, and GUSTAVE GINGRAS. Rehabilitation of the aged. *Canadian Medical Association journal,* v. 93, October 9, 1965: 797-800.

> Discusses goals and objectives of geriatric rehabilitation.

SHORE, HERBERT. The sheltered workshop, does it belong in today's home? *Professional nursing home,* v. 8, February 1966: 14-22.

> An examination of current programs—the pros and cons.

THERAPEUTIC WORKSHOP FOR OLDER PERSONS. Final report. Chicago, Jewish Vocational Service, 1966. 74p. (Monograph no. 5.)

> Points to the relevance of mental health practice to vocational rehabilitation, and to the uses of work in treatment of the emotionally disturbed.

U.S. Dept. of Labor. Office of Manpower Policy, Evaluation, and Research. Sheltered workshops: a pathway to regular employment. Washington, 1967. 36p. (Manpower research bulletin, no. 15.)
Describes the services of sheltered workshops, the clientele they serve, and suggests new directions.

U.S. Office of Vocational Rehabilitation. Report on a study of programs for homebound handicapped individuals. Washington, U.S. Govt. Print. Off., 1955. 123p. (84th Cong., 1st sess., H. doc. no. 98.)
Survey of programs for teaching and training of shut-ins whose disabilities confine them to their homes or beds.

U.S. Vocational Rehabilitation Administration. Standards for rehabilitation facilities and sheltered workshops. Washington, 1967. 17p.
Standards recommended by the National Policy and Performance Council, an advisory body appointed by the Secretary of Health, Education, and Welfare.

Utah University. Graduate School of Social Work. Adjustment of vocational rehabilitation clients. Washington, U.S. Vocational Rehabilitation Administration, 1963. 114p.
Considers social, emotional and physical factors related to vocational rehabilitation adjustment.

White House Conference on Aging. Rehabilitation and aging. A statement of rehabilitation needs, resources, and programs, together with recommendations from the 1961 White House Conference on Aging. Washington, U.S. Govt. Print. Off., 1961. 45p. (Reports and guidelines, series no. 11.)

World Federation of Occupational Therapists. Through youth to age; occupational therapy faces the challenge. Proceedings of the Fourth International Congress . . . Amsterdam, Excerpta Medica Foundation, 1967. 431p. (International congress series no. 135.)
VI. Old age, pp. 241–284.

SOCIAL
and RELATIONSHIP
SOCIAL
ADJUSTMENT

Community Service Activities

CARTER, HOWARD A. The retired senior citizen as a resource to minimize underachievement of children in public schools. *Archives of Physical Medicine and Rehabilitation,* v. 45, May 1964: 218–223.

Project using retired persons to encourage and motivate small groups of selected children within the school setting on a regular weekly basis.

FOLEY, EUGENE P. Counseling small business: a challenge to retired executives. *Aging,* no. 114, April 1964: 1–2; 16.

The administrator of the Small Business Administration describes a questionnaire being sent out.

GREENLEIGH ASSOCIATES. An evaluation of the Foster Grandparent Program. New York, 1966. 89p.

Findings, conclusions and recommendations of the program as it was being carried out in ten local or state-wide projects that were in various stages of development and operation.

LAMBERT, CAMILLE, JR., *and others.* Reopening doors to community participation for older people: how realistic? *Social Service Review,* v. 38, March 1964: 42–50.

Reports a demonstration project to test the feasibility of bringing older persons willing to contribute to the community into those opportunity areas within which their contribution might be made.

MARGOLIS, ELLEN. Grandparents for the asking. *Parents' magazine,* v. 41, December 1966: 60; 104.

MORRIS, ROBERT, *and others.* New roles for the elderly. Waltham, Mass., Florence Heller Graduate School for Advanced Studies in Social Welfare, Brandeis University, 1964. 103p. (Papers in social welfare no. 10.)

Investigation includes manpower potential, opportunities for service, and testing the manpower and the opportunity.

Older people as a resource for service. *Aging,* no. 149, March 1967: 7–10.

Discussion of the Foster Grandparent Program.

PARKE, JAMES H. Enlisting retired elderly persons for volunteer service. *Hospitals,* v. 38, March 16, 1964: 66–68.

The value of older persons in hospital volunteer services.

ROSENBLATT, AARON. Interest of older persons in volunteer activities. *Social Work,* v. 11, July 1966: 87–94.

Discusses program implications in making use of services of 250 older persons who were interviewed about their interest in volunteer work.

———. Older people on the Lower East Side: their interest in employment and volunteer activities and their general characteristics. New York, Dept. of Public Affairs, Community Service Society of New York, 1964. 113p.

Study of the background and capabilities of a selected sample of older persons living on the Lower East Side in New York City.

THUNE, JEANNE, *and others.* Retraining older adults for employment in community services. *Gerontologist,* v. 4, March 1964: 5–9.

Describes a project designed to develop an immediate corps of personnel with adequate training, available as paid or volunteer workers.

U.S. PEACE CORPS. Older volunteers in the Peace Corps. Washington, 1967. n.p.

Describes the jobs more than 150 senior citizens are doing in the Peace Corps.

Who has the greater need? *Aging,* no. 142, August 1966: 7–10.

Summary of Foster Grandparent Program and Projects as of June 1, 1966.

WORTHINGTON, GLADYS. Older persons as community service volunteers. *Social Work,* v. 8, October 1963: 71–75.

Experience of an established volunteer bureau with 197 volunteers of recently retired persons over 65.

Family Life and Intergeneration Relationships

ARTHUR, JULIETTA K. You and yours: how to help older people. Philadelphia, Lippincott, 1960. 315p.

Based on the author's "How to help older people."

BEKKER, L. DeMOYNE, and CHARLES TAYLOR. Attitudes toward the aged in a multi-generational sample. *Journal of Gerontology,* v. 21, January 1966: 115–118.

Comparisons of attitudes toward old age in families which have grandparents with those in families which have grandparents of like age as well as living great-grandparents.

BELL, TONY. The relationship between social involvement and feeling old among residents in homes for the aged. *Journal of Gerontology,* v. 22, January 1967: 17–22.

Disengagement theory furnishes the theoretical background of the study.

122

BELL, WINIFRED. Relatives' responsibility: a problem in social policy. *Social Work*, v. 12, January 1967: 32–39.

    History and background of regulations governing the responsibility of family members for each others support, the provisions now in effect and their inequity.

BENNETT, RUTH. The meaning of institutional life. *Gerontologist*, v. 3, September 1963: 117–125.

    The meaning that institutionalization of the aged has for society, for professional and administrative personnel, for residents of old age institutions, and the sociological meaning of institutional life.

BRODY, ELAINE M. The aging family. *Gerontologist*, v. 6, December 1966: 201–206.

    Survey of family composition of persons applying for admission to a home for the aged over a six-month period.

————. Aging is a family affair. *Public Welfare*, v. 25, April 1967: 129–132; 137.

    Some of the restrictive policies in public welfare agencies that make it difficult for the aged and their families to maintain strong relationships.

————, and GERALDINE M. SPARK. Institutionalization of the aged: a family crisis. *Family Process*, v. 5, March 1966: 76–90.

    Presents and discusses illustrative case material in examining the request for institutionalization in terms of its familial implications.

BRUDNO, JOSEPH J. Group programs with adult offspring of newly admitted residents in a geriatric setting. *Journal of the American Geriatrics Society*, v. 12, April 1964: 385–394.

    Program to improve the adjustment of children to the placement of parents in a geriatric institution.

COAKLEY, MARY LEWIS. When parents grow old. Pulaski, Wisconsin, Franciscan Publishers, 1967. 64p.

    Discusses living arrangements, physical and mental conditions, and offers constructive action.

COALE, ANSLEY J., *and others*. Aspects of the analysis of family structure. Princeton, Princeton University Press, 1965. 248p.

    Views of five prominent scholars on concepts of kinship structure and the family unit.

CONFERENCE ON GERONTOLOGY. The older person in the family: challenges and conflicts. Proceedings . . . Iowa City, Iowa, Institute of Gerontology, University of Iowa, 1965. 71p.

    The role of the older person in the family.

DEAN, STANLEY R. Sin and senior citizens. *Journal of the American Geriatrics Society*, v. 14, September 1966: 935–938.

    Social security problems of remarriage for widows.

Duvall, Evelyn Millis. Family development. Philadelphia, Lippincott, 1957. 533p.

> Part III. Contracting families. Chapter 12. Families in the middle years. Chapter 14. Aging families.

Egerman, Leonard E. Attitudes of adult children toward parents and parents' problems. *Geriatrics,* v. 21, June 1966: 217–222.

> Adult children may have problems that hinder their own ability to care for their geriatric parents.

Family Service Association of America. The family is all generations. New York, 1965. 46p.

> Ways of helping older people and their families.

Farber, Seymour M., *and others,* eds. Man and civilization; the family's search for survival. New York, McGraw-Hill, 1965. 210p.

> The intimate relations of older people, by *Alvin I. Goldfarb,* p. 183–196.

Feldman, Frances L. The family in a money world. New York, Family Service Association of America, 1957. 188p.

> The family, its needs, its income, and its social adjustments to a rising standard of living within a monetary system.

Hart, Mollie. When your husband retires. New York, Appleton, 1960. 172p.

> Points out what areas may require mutual adjustment and what the advantages of retirement can be.

Kalish, Richard A. Of children and grandfathers: a speculative essay on dependency. *Gerontologist,* v. 7, March 1967: 65–69; 79.

> "Ways in which the values internalized by the elderly person *himself* degrade his role in his own eyes."

Liebman, Samuel, ed. Emotional forces in the family. Philadelphia, Lippincott, 1959. 157p.

> Chapter 6. The impact of aging in the family, by *D. Griffith McKarracher.*

Miller, Michael B., and Audrey P. Harris. The chronically ill aged: paradoxical patient-family behavior. *Journal of the American Geriatrics Society,* v. 15, May 1965: 480–495.

> Study of the effect of the patient's behavior on the family and the effect of the family's behavior on the patient during the adaptation period of the admission of a chronically ill aged patient to a nursing home.

———, ———. Family cognizance of disability in the aged on nursing home placement. *Social Casework,* v. 45, March 1964: 150–154.

> Study of family awareness of the patient's disability in the cases of 90 patients, those in residence in January 1963 and those admitted between January and June 1963.

MILLER, MICHAEL B., and AUDREY P. HARRIS. Social factors and family conflicts in a nursing home population. *Journal of the American Geriatrics Society*, v. 13, September 1965: 845–851.
Study to determine patient's living arrangements six months before, and immediately prior to placement in the nursing home.

NEW JERSEY. DIVISION ON AGING. The multi-generation family; papers on theory and practice, problems and promise. Trenton, 1964. 22p.
Older people and their families, by *Ethel Shanas*. Filial responsibility from the point of view of the private agency, by *Theodore R. Isenstadt*. Filial responsibility from the point of view of a public agency, by *Margaret Barnard*. General statements on legally responsible relatives—New Jersey public welfare point of view, by *Gertrude Lotwin*.

PRESTON, CAROLINE E., and KAREN S. GUDIKSEN. A measure of self-perception among older people. *Journal of Gerontology*, v. 21, January 1966: 63–71.
Development of techniques to explore the different ways in which old people see their world and themselves.

RICHARDSON, FRANK HOWARD. Grandparents and their families: a guide for three generations. New York, McKay, 1964. 116p.
The way to a happier relationship among grandparents, parents, and the grandchildren.

ROSOW, IRVING. The aged, family and friends. *Social Security Bulletin*, v. 28, November 1965: 18–20.
Relationship of older persons to their children and friends.

SCHORR, ALVIN L. Filial responsibility in the modern American family: an evaluation of current practice of filial responsibility in the United States and the relationship to it of social security programs. Washington, U.S. Govt. Print. Off., 1960. 45p.

SHANAS, ETHEL. Family help patterns and social class in three countries. *Journal of Marriage and the Family*, v. 29, May 1967: 257–266.
Help patterns among older people and their adult children in Denmark, Britain, and the U.S.

———. Family relationships of older people; living arrangements, health status, and family ties, as reported by the aged, the persons to whom they would turn in a health crisis, and the general public. New York, Health Information Foundation, 1961. 64p. (HIF research series No. 20.)

SOLOMON, BARBARA. Social functioning of economically dependent aged. *Gerontologist*, v. 7, September 1967, Pt. I: 213–217.
Analysis of a random sample of economically dependent, aged persons to determine whether there were personal and environmental factors associated with the experience of life satisfaction.

STERN, EDITH M., and MABEL ROSS. You and your aging parents. Rev. and enl. ed. New York, Harper, 1965. 211p.

STREIB, GORDON F. Intergenerational relations: perspectives of the two generations on the older parent. *Journal of Marriage and the Family*, v. 27, November 1965: 469–476.
  Focus on the family life of elderly retired males and the way in which these men and their adult children perceive certain phases of family life.

SULLIVAN, MARY E. A study of discharge planning for older hospitalized veterans. *Geriatrics*, v. 20, September 1965: 778–782.
  Study reveals that patients were eager to return home after treatment, and did not experience family rejection, loss of pride, or pessimism for the future.

SYMPOSIUM ON THE FAMILY, INTERGENERATIONAL RELATIONS AND SOCIAL STRUCTURE. Social structure and the family: generational relations. Englewood Cliffs, N.J., Prentice-Hall, 1965. 394p.
  Cross-cultural perspective of the three-generation family structure in Western society with emphasis on generational relationships of older family members.

TOWNSEND, PETER. The family life of old people; an inquiry in East London. London, Routledge and Kegan Paul, 1957. 284p.
  Account of the social anatomy of successful family life, the environmental factors and the internal adaptations necessary to bind one generation with another.

TUNSTALL, JEREMY. Old and alone; a sociological study of old people. London, Routledge, 1966. 344p.
  Statistical analysis of four types of aloneness: living alone, lonely, socially isolated, and anomic.

YOUMANS, E. GRANT. Family disengagement among older urban and rural women. *Journal of Gerontology*, v. 22, April 1967: 209–211.
  Concerned with family visiting patterns and family helping relationships.

Life in Retirement and Retirement Preparation Programs

AMEND, DEXTER R. A critical appraisal of retirement programs in Washington state. *Geriatrics*, v. 20, October 1965: 885–888.

AMERICAN ASSOCIATION OF RETIRED PERSONS. A report on preparation for retirement in the federal government. Washington, 1967. Various paging.
  Based on responses to questionnaires sent to every agency of the executive branch of the federal government.

ANDERSON, NANCY N. Effects of institutionalization on self-esteem. *Journal of Gerontology,* v. 22, July 1967: 313–317.

Evaluation of the effects of retirement home living on the self-esteem of the residents.

ASH, PHILIP. Pre-retirement counseling. *Gerontologist,* v. 6, June 1966: 97–99; 127–128.

Describes results of a ten-year study and gives main steps in a pre-retirement counseling program.

BAUDER, WARD W. Farmers' definitions of retirement. *Gerontologist,* v. 7, September 1967, Pt. I: 207–212.

Data on farmers' views of retirement obtained from a 10% area-probability sample of farm operators in 2 counties and ½ of a third county in eastern South Dakota.

BELL, JESSE G. Retirement counseling enhances pension program values. *Pension and Welfare News,* v. 2, March 1966: 47–48.

Case examples of several programs.

BORTZ, EDWARD L. Retirement and the individual. *Journal of the American Geriatrics Society,* v. 16, January 1968: 1–15.

Focuses on the quality of living in the post-retirement years.

BRAY, GEORGE A. What Illinois Bell has learned from its retirement planning program. *Personnel,* v. 41, November-December 1964: 37–42.

BUCKLEY, JOSEPH C. The retirement handbook. 3rd ed. New York, Harper, 1967. 362p.

Retirement planning guide.

BURGESS, ERNEST W. Retirement preparation: Chicago plan. Washington, U.S. Govt. Print. Off., 1961. 10p. (Patterns for progress in aging, case study no. 5.)

Study of the University of Chicago's retirement planning and preparation program.

COOLEY, LELAND FREDERICK, and LEE MORRISON COOLEY. The retirement trap. Garden City, N.Y., Doubleday, 1965. 184p.

Behind-the-scenes look at retirement living.

DONAHUE, WILMA T., and CLARK TIBBITTS, eds. Planning the older years. Ann Arbor, University of Michigan Press, 1950. 248p.

Organized around the areas of living arrangements, recreational activities, and employment.

DUFFUS, R. L. Adventure in retirement. New York, Norton, 1965. 270p.

What to do when you no longer have to do anything.

FIELDS, CHRIS L. Behind the curtain of retirement. Philadelphia, Dorrance, 1966. 26p.

Discusses problems that beset retirees, including the causes of the problems and the solutions.

FLINT, HELEN M., and TED RUHIG. Planning for retirement; a university-labor union program. Washington, U.S. Govt. Print. Off., 1964. 17p. (Patterns for progress in aging case study no. 16.)

Describes the pre-retirement program created by the Labor Division of Roosevelt University, Chicago, and Local 1859 of the International Brotherhood of Electrical Workers.

GALLAWAY, LOWELL E. The retirement decision: an exploratory essay. Washington, U.S. Govt. Print. Off., 1965. 62p. (Research report no. 9.)

Analysis of the economics of the decision elderly people face upon reaching retirement age.

HAVIGHURST, ROBERT J., *and others*. A cross-national study of adjustment to retirement. *Gerontologist,* v. 6, September 1966, Pt. I: 137–138.

Description of a comparative study being made by a group of social scientists from seven countries.

JOELSON, JACK B., and DAVID RACHLIS. Anticipating the consequences of aging: a pilot program in adult education. *Journal of Jewish Communal Service,* v. 41, Summer 1965: 369–377.

Describes development, execution, and evaluation of a retirement planning program by and for the Jewish community of Pittsburgh.

KERCKHOFF, ALAN C. Husband-wife expectations and reactions to retirement. *Journal of Gerontology,* v. 19, October 1964: 510–516.

Compares husband-wife responses before and after retirement.

LEGLER, HENRY. How to make the rest of your life the best of your life. New York, Simon, 1967. 351p.

How to find the interests and activities that will suit you best.

LIPMAN, AARON, and PHILIP W. MARDEN. Preparation for death in old age. *Journal of Gerontology,* v. 21, July 1966: 426–431.

Study to discover the extent to which retired persons living in public housing had made provisions for death.

LUNDGREN, EARL F. Compatibility of a successful work experience with retirement. *Mental Hygiene,* v. 50, July 1966: 463–467.

Concludes that companies have a responsibility to train workers for retirement just as beginning workers are trained for their jobs.

———. Needed—retirement counseling programs in business. *Personnel Journal,* v. 44, September 1965: 432–436.

Deals with company counseling of employees facing retirement in anywhere from one day to five or ten years or more.

128

MOORE, ELON H. The nature of retirement. New York, Macmillan, 1959. 217p.

Guidepost for facing retirement. Includes brief case histories and covers both the biological and social aspects of retirement.

ODELL, CHARLES E. An urgent need: education for retirement. *AFL–CIO American Federationist,* v. 73, September 1966: 21–24.

Describes the UAW-Scoville plan.

OTTO, HERBERT. Research on human potentialities: application to geriatric programs. *Journal of the American Geriatrics Society,* v. 12, July 1964: 677–686.

Concludes that retirement preparation programs need to reach the potential retiree years before his actual retirement.

PALMORE, ERDMAN B. Differences in the retirement patterns of men and women. *Gerontologist,* v. 5, March 1965, Pt. I: 4–8.

Analyzes data from the *1963 Survey of the Aged* and discusses its relation to role theory.

PITKIN, WALTER, JR. Life begins at fifty. New York, Simon, 1965. 224p.

Personal observations and testimony of many people.

PRASAD, S. BENJAMIN. The retirement postulate of the disengagement theory. *Gerontologist,* v. 4, March 1964: 20–23.

THE RETIREMENT COUNCIL, INC. Retirement money guidebook. New York, Harper, 1963. 126p.

I. Lay the groundwork for financial security. II. What you can do to remain financially secure. III. Part-time jobs and second careers.

————. Retirement planning guidebook. Stamford, Conn., 1958. 96p.

SELIN, BERT W. So you're going to retire; good planning—prelude to happiness. New York, Vantage, 1964. 53p.

Suggestions on where to live; health principles; psychology for the older person; creative projects.

STERN, EDITH M. A full life after 65. New York, Public Affairs Committee, 1963. 28p. (Public affairs pamphlet, no. 347.)

Discusses psychological and practical problems people face after retirement.

STOKES, RANDALL G., and GEORGE L. MADDOX. Some social factors in retirement adaptation. *Journal of Gerontology,* v. 22, 1967: 329–333.

"Relationship of occupational prestige, the intrinsic meaning of the work career, and the length of time retired to adaptation in retirement."

U.S. SOCIAL SECURITY ADMINISTRATION. Planning for the later years. Washington, U.S. Govt. Print. Off., 1967. 51p.

Developed from digests of talks given during a series of seminars on retirement planning.

WEBBER, IRVING L., ed. Aging and retirement. Gainesville, University of Florida Press, 1955. 142p. (Institute of Gerontology series no. 5)

Report on the fifth annual Southern Conference on Gerontology held at the University of Florida, December 28–30, 1954.

WERMEL, MICHAEL T., and GERALDINE M. BEIDEMAN. Retirement preparation programs: a study of company responsibilities. Pasadena, Calif., Institute of Technology, 1961. 194p.

Shows what management should and can do to help employees with their retirement planning.

WRIGHT, CLARENCE. Successful retirement: plan it now. Washington, Kiplinger Washington Editors, 1965. 96p.

Plans to be made, problems to be solved, decisions that will affect you and your family in the future.

ZIMMERMAN, GEREON. The secret of successful retirement. New York, Simon and Schuster, 1962. 352p.

Places special emphasis on the financial aspects of retirement. Special section describes facilities for older people in American communities.

Recreation, Creative Activity, Education, Religion, and Political Action

BASS, IRVING. Personnel for activity and recreation programs: qualifications and function. *Journal of the American Geriatrics Society*, v. 13, May 1965: 442–446.

Suggestions for improving the situation for clarifying the qualifications and duties of recreation workers in programs for the aged, handicapped, and chronically ill.

BEHNKE, CHARLES A. Today and tomorrow; devotions for people who are growing with the years. St. Louis, Concordia, 1965. 120p.

Meditations, prayers, and hymns.

BELTER, E. W. What does the church expect for its aging? *Professional Nursing Home*, v. 6, February 1964: 30–34.

"The church is concerned with the total environment of the total creature."

BORCHARDT, MARJORIE V. A senior citizens association. Washington, U.S. Govt. Print. Off., 1961. 22p. (Patterns for progress in aging, case study no. 6.)

Evaluation of the Senior Citizens Association of Los Angeles County, Inc.

BRIGHTBILL, CHARLES K. Educating for leisure-centered living. Harrisburg, Pa., Stackpole, 1966. 232p.

Comprehensive interpretation of leisure.

BROSS, DOROTHY R. Night college courses for the older woman. *Adult Leadership*, v. 15, January 1967: 233–234.

Help in filling the need of the older woman to communicate.

BURNS, HOBERT W., ed. Sociological backgrounds of adult education. Chicago, Center for the Study of Liberal Education for Adults, 1964. 169p. (Notes and essays on education for adults, no. 41.)

A group of sociologists summarize pertinent research in the areas of demography, social change, adult status and roles, adult value changes, and adult uses of education.

CONFERENCE ON THE ROLE OF EDUCATION FOR AGING AND THE AGED. Proceedings, November 30-December 2, 1961, at the Center for Continuation Study, University of Minnesota, Minneapolis, n.d. 91p.

Purpose of conference to help states in region VI of the U.S. Department of Health, Education, and Welfare to develop programs for conferences on education for aging.

CONFERENCE ON THE ROLE OF EDUCATION IN THE FIELD OF AGING. Proceedings, November 27 and 28, 1961. Charlottesville, Va., University of Virginia, various paging.

Conference held by the Division of Extension and General Studies of the University of Virginia in cooperation with region III of the U.S. Department of Health, Education, and Welfare.

————, UNIVERSITY OF MARYLAND, 1962. State leadership in action for education in aging. Washington, U.S. Office of Aging and U.S. Office of Education, 1963. 54p. (OA no. 119.)

Follow-up conference held in September 1962. Summaries, recommendations, and key speeches.

COSGROVE, ROBERT C. It's never too late. *Music Journal*, v. 24; September 1966: 35; 84.

Briefly describes a music education project sponsored by the National Council on the Aging.

CURTIS, JOSEPH E., and DULCY B. MILLER. Community sponsored recreation in an extended care facility. *Gerontologist*, v. 7, September 1967, Pt. I: 196–199, 224.

Program developed to meet the need of the aged in a suburban community.

DELVALLE, JUNE, *and others.* Reading patterns of the aged in a nursing home environment. *Professional Nursing Home*, v. 7, June 1965: 46–53.

Describes a program begun by a public library as a service to patients in a nursing home.

131

DESROCHES, HARRY F., *and others.* Age and leisure-time activities in a VA domiciliary. *Geriatrics,* v. 20, December 1965: 1065–1069.

In a study concerned with the relationship between age and leisure-time activity in an aged, institutionalized population, it was found that other factors may be more associated with leisure-time activity than age.

DIXON, J. C., ed. Continuing education in the later years. Gainesville, University of Florida Press, 1963. 124p.

Report on the 12th annual Southern Conference on Gerontology held at the University of Florida, February 21–22, 1963.

DONAHUE, WILMA T., comp. Education for later maturity; a handbook. New York, Whiteside, 1955. 338p.

Reports of educational activities for the aging and their evaluation. Compiled under the auspices of the Adult Education Association of the United States of America.

————, and CLARK TIBBETTS, eds. Politics of age: proceedings of the University of Michigan 14th annual conference on aging. Ann Arbor, University of Michigan, Division of Gerontology, 1962. 226p.

Examines political implications of the increasing number of older people in the U.S.

————, *and others,* eds. Free time; challenge to later maturity. Ann Arbor, University of Michigan Press, 1958. 172p.

Selection of papers presented at the University of Michigan's tenth anniversary conference on aging.

GRATTAN, C. HARTLEY, ed. American ideas about adult education, 1710–1951. New York, Teachers College, Columbia University, 1959. 140p. (Classics in education no. 2.)

Selected expositions of points of view closely related to actual undertakings in the field.

GRAY, ROBERT M., and DAVID O. MOBERG. The church and the older person. Grand Rapids, Eerdman, 1962. 162p.

Place and function of religion in the lives of older persons.

GRUBER, FREDERICK C., ed. Education in transition; 47th annual school-men's week proceedings. Philadelphia, University of Pennsylvania Press, 1960. 278p.

"Constructive leadership with the aging conference report," by *Philip A. Boyer,* p. 44–51.

Handbook of adult education in the United States. Chicago, Adult Education Association of the U.S.A.

Published irregularly.

HANNAN, JOSEPH F. Killing time. New York, Holt, 1964. 164p.

What to do with leisure time.

HENDRICKSON, ANDREW, and ROBERT F. BARNES. Educational needs of older people. *Adult Leadership,* v. 16, May 1967: 2–4; 32.

Study, conducted within the city limits of Columbus, Ohio, to determine the educational needs of older people.

HOGE, EVELYN BROWN. Developing clubs for older people. Chicago, American Public Welfare Association, 1954. 15p. (How public welfare serves aging people, no. 3.)

INSTITUTE ON LIBRARY SERVICE TO AN AGING POPULATION. Library service to an aging population. Chicago, American Library Association, 1960. 60p.

An institute presented by the Adult Services Division and the Office for Adult Education of the American Library Association, June 22–26, 1959. Edited by *Ruth M. White.*

JOHNSON, GERALD K. Spiritual aspects of aging. *Lutheran Social Welfare Quarterly,* v. 4, September 1964: 28–36.

JOHNSTONE, JOHN W. C., and RAMON J. RIVERA. Volunteers for learning; a study of the educational pursuits of American adults. Chicago, Aldine, 1965. 624p.

Overview of contemporary adult education, from a social-psychological vantage point, on the needs, motives, and satisfactions which impel adults to seek to learn some subject.

KAPLAN, MAX. Leisure in America: a social inquiry. New York, Wiley, 1960. 350p.

Analyzes leisure and discusses patterns of leisure activity in today's American society.

KENNEDY, ALICE. Specialized services for geriatric patients. *Nursing Homes,* v. 14, June 1965: 5–8.

Discusses creative activity for the treatment of older people who are ill, in the prevention of their illnesses, and in the after-care following illness.

KENT, DONALD P. Current developments in educational programming for older people. *American School Board Journal,* v. 149, September 1964: 27; 30.

Outlines some of the dimensions of education and aging and indicates some successful programs in operation.

KIDD, JAMES ROBBINS. How adults learn. New York, Association Press, 1959. 324p.

Discusses capacities, physical and intellectual; emotions; motivations; theories of learning; methods of teaching.

KLEEMEIER, ROBERT WATSON, ed. Aging and leisure; a research perspective into the meaningful use of time. New York, Oxford University Press, 1961. 447p.

KNAPP, MARK L. Speech education for the aged. *Speech Teacher,* v. 13, November 1964: 299–303.

Discusses existing programs.

KOCH, MOSES S., and SAUL E. LILIENSTEIN. A community college attracts the aging. *Junior College Journal,* v. 35, October 1964: 26–27.

Describes a program designed to attract the senior citizen into the college classroom.

KREPS, JUANITA M. Lifetime allocation of work and leisure. Washington, U.S. Govt. Print. Off., 1968. 44p. (Research report no. 22.)

Comparisons between the work and leisure pattern of the U.S., with its growing tendency toward retirement below age 65, and the patterns of certain Western European countries.

KUHLEN, RAYMOND G., ed. Psychological backgrounds of adult education. Chicago, Center for the Study of Liberal Education for Adults, 1964. 148p. Notes and essays on education for adults, no. 40.)

Participants in a conference discuss adult capacities to learn, personality changes and motivational changes during the adult years, and psychological characteristics of adults and instructional methods in adult education.

KURASIK, STEVE. The need for recreational therapy in hospitals, nursing homes and homes for the aged. *Journal of the American Geriatrics Society,* v. 13, June 1965: 556–560.

Results of a questionnaire survey of 16 federal hospitals in New York and New Jersey and 14 private hospitals in the Capital District of New York State, and personal visits to 10 nursing homes in the Capital District.

———, and RODERICK O'CONNOR. Why recreation in hospitals, nursing homes and homes for the aged? *Journal of the American Geriatrics Society,* v. 14, June 1966: 643–646.

Discusses need for recreation in general hospitals, nursing homes, and community and voluntary homes.

LENZER, ANTHONY. The role of the university in gerontological training. *Gerontologist,* v. 6, June 1966: 105–110.

Describes potential roles in lay and professional education on aging, including the aging themselves.

LEWIS, AUGUSTUS. Attitudes of geriatric patients toward planned activity. *Geriatrics,* v. 18, September 1963: 725–728.

LUCAS, CAROL. Recreation in gerontology. Springfield, Ill., Thomas, 1964. 177p.

Practical guide for establishing or expanding programs of activity for older people.

LUCAS, CAROL, ed. Recreational activity development for the aging in homes, hospitals and nursing homes. Springfield, Ill., Thomas, 1962. 59p.

Guide to establish effective programs and provide stimuli for existing programs.

LYON, MARY, ed. Crafts for retirement, rev. ed. New York, American Craftsmen's Council, 1964. 134p.

Guidebook for teachers and students.

MADOW, PAULINE, ed. Recreation in America. New York, H. W. Watson, 1965. 206p. (Reference shelf, vol. 37, no. 2.)

Information and comments on the social and economic effects of increased leisure in America and the role of public agencies in providing recreational facilities.

MARYLAND COMMISSION ON THE AGING CONFERENCE. State leadership in action for education in aging; proceedings, September 6-7, 1962. Washington, U.S. Department of Health, Education, and Welfare, 1963. 54p.

Summaries, recommendations, and key speeches.

MAVES, PAUL B. Older people and the church. New York, Abingdon-Cokesbury Press, 1949. 272p.

MAY, SIEGMUND H. Purposeful mass activity; a provocative experiment with the aged. *Geriatrics,* v. 21, October 1966: 193-200.

Describes a project initiated by a home for the aged.

MERRILL, TONI. Activities for the aged and infirm; a handbook for the untrained worker. Springfield, Ill., Thomas, 1967. 372p.

The why, how, what, when, and where of organizing and conducting appropriate programs for the aged and infirm.

MEYER, HAROLD D., and CHARLES K. BRIGHTBILL. Community recreation; a guide to its organization. 3rd ed. Englewood Cliffs, N.J., Prentice-Hall, 1964. 461p.

I. Background. II. Recreation and government. III. Recreation and the social institutions. IV. Recreation in other settings. V. Recreation for special groups.

MOBERG, DAVID O. Religion in old age. *Geriatrics,* v. 20, November, 1965: 977-982.

"To be as effective as possible, the physician must recognize the role of religion in health, illness, and therapy."

———. Religiosity in old age. *Gerontologist,* v. 5, June 1965: 78-87; 111.

Describes Professor Glock's classification of "dimensions of religiosity" and summarizes some findings from studies about religion in old age.

MULAC, MARGARET E. Leisure time for living and retirement. New York, Harper, 1961. 213p.

> Problems of aging and retirement are also problems of the individual's early life. Shows ways to develop creative pursuits.

NASH, JAY B. Recreation: pertinent readings. Dubuque, Iowa, Wm. C. Brown, 1965. 265p.

> History and philosophy of recreation along with present and future trends and the interests of federal, state, and local governments.

NATIONAL RECREATION ASSOCIATION. CONSULTING SERVICE ON RECREATION FOR THE ILL AND HANDICAPPED. Recreation for the handicapped in the community setting. New York, 1965. 39p.

> A guide for community recreation departments, neighborhood centers and other agencies concerned with the recreation needs of the handicapped.

NEW YORK (STATE) UNIVERSITY. STATE EDUCATION DEPARTMENT. STATE RECREATION COUNCIL FOR THE ELDERLY. A decade of recreation for the elderly, 1956–1966. Albany, 1968. 34p.

> Report on the programs of educational-recreational activities adapted to the needs of older persons.

PINNER, FRANK A., and others. Old age and political behavior; a case study. Berkeley and Los Angeles, University of California Press, 1959. 352p.

> Deals with the California Institute of Social Welfare, a political pressure group composed chiefly of recipients of old age assistance, approximately 20 percent of the aged on California's public welfare rolls.

REINGOLD, JACOB. Octogenarians work for a living in three-year health-morale study. *Hospitals,* v. 38, September 16, 1964: 59–65.

> Research program at a home for the aged that seeks to revive elderly persons' interest in life through gainful employment.

RETIREMENT COUNCIL, ed. 101 ways to enjoy your leisure. Stamford, Conn., 1963. 125p.

> Illustrated guide to low-cost freetime activities and opportunities for service, fun, education, and exercise.

SCUDDER, DELTON L., ed. Organized religion and the older person. Gainesville, University of Florida Press, 1958. 113p. (Institute of gerontology series no. 8.)

> Report on the eighth annual Southern Conference on Gerontology held at the University of Florida, April 10–11, 1958.

STEIN, WALTER. Try an amateur radio station. *Professional Nursing Home,* v. 8, July 1966: 18–20.

> Describes the installation of an amateur radio station in a nursing home.

THOMPSON, MORTON. Starting a recreation program in institutions for the ill or handicapped aged. New York, National Recreation Association, 1960. 28p.

TWENTE, ESTHER E. Aging, strength, and creativity. *Social Work*, v. 10, July 1965: 105–110.
Sketches of men and women in small communities and their hobbies.

U.S. NATIONAL ADVISORY COMMITTEE FOR THE WHITE HOUSE CONFERENCE ON AGING. Background paper on free-time activities: recreation, voluntary services, citizenship participation. Washington, U.S. Govt. Print. Off., 1960. (Background paper no. 12.)

U.S. OFFICE OF EDUCATION. Educationally deficient adults; their education and training needs. Washington, U.S. Govt. Print. Off., 1965. 60p.
Survey to organize pertinent information about, and to develop guidelines for, a solution to the occupational training problems faced by unskilled, undereducated, unemployed adults.

U.S. OUTDOOR RECREATION RESOURCES REVIEW COMMISSION. National recreation survey. Washington, U.S. Govt. Print. Off., 1962. 394p. (ORRRC study report 19.)
Tabular results and analyses of a nationwide survey of the outdoor recreation habits and preferences of the American people 12 years of age and over.

———. Participation in outdoor recreation: factors affecting demand among American adults. Washington, U.S. Govt. Print. Off., 1962. 94p. (ORRRC study report 20.)
Results of a survey conducted by the Survey Research Center, University of Michigan. Discusses the effect upon participation of income, education, occupation, paid vacations, place of residence, region, sex, age, life cycle, and race.

U.S. WOMEN'S BUREAU. Continuing education programs for women. Washington, U.S. Govt. Print. Off., 1966. 31p. (Pamphlet no. 10.)
Report prepared for college educators and administrators and for mature women who want to return to school or work after a period devoted to homemaking and desire to refresh skills learned 10 to 20 years earlier.

WHITE HOUSE CONFERENCE ON AGING. Free-time activities; recreation, voluntary service, citizenship participation. A statement of needs, values, and importance of free-time activities to individual and social well-being of senior citizens together with recommendations from the 1961 White House Conference on Aging. Washington, U.S. Govt. Print. Off., 1961. 64p. (Reports and guidelines, series no. 6.)

WILLIAMS, ARTHUR. Recreation in the senior years. New York, Association Press, 1962. 252p.
Revision of "Recreation for the aging."

ZARITZKY, SONJA, and H. GRAUER. Development of an out-patient geriatric occupational therapy programme in a Montreal hospital, 1960–1966. *Journal of the American Geriatrics Society,* v. 15, May 1965: 496–501.

Experience showed that elderly disengaged patients can overcome their isolation and depression with the proper individual and group support in the proper setting.

ZOLLINGER, HELEN. A community craft program. Washington, U.S. Govt. Print. Off., 1961. 12p. (Patterns for progress in aging, case study no. 4.)

Describes program of Senior Craftsmen of Oregon, Inc.

SOCIAL
and
ENVIRONMENTAL
SERVICES

Church Programs and Services

BOE, PAUL A. The obligation of the church in social welfare. *Lutheran Social Welfare Quarterly*, v. 3, September 1963: 14–20.

Areas of organization necessary on the part of the church to provide the framework within which concern for the needs of people can be expressed.

BOYLAN, MARGUERITE T., ed. The Catholic Church and social welfare; a symposium. New York, Greenwich Book Publishers, 1961. 217p.

BROWN, J. PAUL. Counseling with senior citizens. Englewood Cliffs, N.J., Prentice-Hall, 1964. 144p.

Drawn from personal experience, intended to provide the minister with practical help in working with older people.

COUGHLIN, BERNARD J. Church and state in social welfare. New York, Columbia University Press, 1965. 189p.

Study of the role of voluntary welfare in the nation's total welfare program.

CROSS, JAMES C., and JOHN M. MASON. Are Lutherans placing too much emphasis on homes for the aged?: a dialogue. *Lutheran Social Welfare Quarterly*, v. 4, December 1964: 28–41.

Two panelists present their reasons why they think the American Lutheran Church is not placing too much emphasis on homes for the aged.

CULVER, ELSIE THOMAS. New church programs with the aging. New York, Association Press, 1961. 152p.

Discusses role of the church in relation to the older people in the community.

DOBBINS, GAINES STANLEY. The years ahead. Nashville, Convention Press, 1959. 144p.

One of the books used in the church study course for teaching by the Baptist Church.

DOUGLAS, MARGARET. Serving the lonely aging. *Catholic Charities Review*, v. 49, April 1965: 13–16.

Program of the San Francisco Archdiocesan Catholic Committee for the Aging in assisting the elderly to remain self-sufficient in their own homes.

GLEASON, GEORGE. Horizons for older people. New York, Macmillan, 1956. 137p.

How the church can help meet the needs of the older adults in the community.

INTERNATIONAL CONFERENCE ON THE CHURCH AND OLDER PERSONS. The fulfillment years in Christian education; the older adult program. Chicago, Department of Education and Distribution, National Council of Churches of Christ in the United States of America, 1953. 32p.

JACOBS, H. LEE. Senior citizens in the church and community. 3d ed. Iowa City, Iowa, State University of Iowa, 1960. 42p.

Roles of the church and community in retirement planning.

JEWISH FEDERATION OF METROPOLITAN CHICAGO. Report on services to the aged. Chicago, 1966. 217p. and suppl.

Institutional and non-institutional services provided by the Federation. 14-page supplement briefly describes governmental programs affecting aged individuals.

JOHNSON, F. ERNEST, ed. Religion and social work. New York, Harper, 1956. 194p.

Chapter VIII. "Religion and the aged," by *Catherine Lee Wallstrom.*

MILLER, HASKELL M. Compassion and community; an appraisal of the church's changing role in social welfare. New York, Association Press, 1961. 288p.

Historical role of the churches and their relation to the new social welfare needs of people; relationship of the church to social work and the social worker; needs and services in special areas of the church's concern.

NATIONAL CONFERENCE ON THE CHURCHES AND SOCIAL WELFARE. Report. New York, Friendship Press.

First conference held in 1955 and a smaller delegated group meeting in 1957. Second conference held in 1961.

NATIONAL COUNCIL OF THE EPISCOPAL CHURCH. Report on retirement housing in the Episcopal Church. New York, 1964. 42p.

How other denominations are working in the field of retirement housing and what the Episcopal Church is doing. Explores samples of how retirement homes operate.

RANDALL, OLLIE A. Philosophy of serving the aged. *Lutheran Social Welfare Quarterly,* v. 4, September 1964: 37–44.

"The author states that the church, through its organizations, may well be the one place where man can be treated 'whole'."

142

RISMILLER, ARTHUR P. Older members in the congregation. Minneapolis, Augsberg, 1964. 127p.

Material to be used as a guide by churches in their programs of services to older members.

STEER, H. P. Caring for the elderly. London, S.P.C.K., 1966. 106p.

Church work with the aged.

STOUGH, ADA BARNETT. Brighter vistas; the story of four church programs for older adults. Washington, U.S. Govt. Print. Off., 1965. 52p. (Patterns for progress in aging case study no. 18.)

Older adult programs at St. Luke's Methodist Church in Oklahoma City, Okla.; First Baptist Church in Los Angeles, Cal.; Riverside Church in New York City; and First Methodist Church in Baton Rouge, La.

U.S. NATIONAL ADVISORY COMMITTEE FOR THE WHITE HOUSE CONFERENCE ON AGING. Background paper on religion and aging. Washington, U.S. Govt. Print. Off., 1960. 24p. (Background paper no. 13.)

WHITE HOUSE CONFERENCE ON AGING. Religion and aging. A report of the problems and issues together with the recommendation and policy statements from the White House Conference on Aging. Washington, U.S. Govt. Print. Off., 1961. 22p. (Reports and guidelines, series no. 7.)

Community Planning and Organization

BAYNE, J. RONALD. Illness and age. *Canadian Welfare*, v. 43, March-April 1967: 14–18.

An approach in community service in geriatrics.

BENNETT, LOUIS L. Protective services for the aged. *Social Service Review*, v. 39, September 1965: 283–293.

Discusses the planning of a community protective service program.

BRUYN, SEVERYN T. Communities in action; pattern and process. New Haven, Conn., College and University Press, 1963. 205p.

Focuses on what happened in four Illinois towns when the local population followed contemporary models of community action to solve their problems.

BUELL, BRADLEY, *and others*. Community planning for human services. New York, Columbia University Press, 1952. 464p.

Complex problems of human trouble from the perspective of the local community. Summarized in Walton, Eloise. Let's work together in community service. New York, Public Affairs Committee, 1953. 28p. (Public Affairs pamphlet no. 194.)

CASO, ELIZABETH K., and HARRY T. PHILLIPS. Small-grants projects in Massachusetts for the chronically ill and aged. *Public Health Reports,* v. 81, May 1966: 471–477.

Describes a network of community services evolving from a small-grants program of the division of adult health of the Massachusetts Department of Public Health.

CENTRAL BUREAU FOR THE JEWISH AGED. A community looks at its practices for improving services to the mentally impaired aging. New York, 1965. 48p.

Proceedings of a conference held in October, 1964.

CLARK, DEAN A. Organizing community health services for the aged. *Hospitals,* v. 40, January 16, 1966: 52–56.

Review of problems of establishing a medical care program for the aged, with suggested course of action.

CONFERENCE OF STATE EXECUTIVES ON AGING. Meeting needs of older persons where they live; the state's role in community planning and action. Washington, U.S. Govt. Print. Off., 1964. 97p.

Selected papers from the conference held April 22–24, 1963.

CONFERENCE ON URBAN PUBLIC WELFARE ADMINISTRATION. Restructuring public welfare administration to meet the needs of people in an urban society. Report. Washington, U.S. Welfare Administration, 1966. 16p.

Restructuring specifically related to: federal, state and local relationships; effective delivery of services to people in the urban community; role, function, and attitude of public welfare staff; and community relations.

DUNHAM, ARTHUR. Community welfare organization: principles and practice. New York, Crowell, 1958. 480p.

Part I. Background material. Part II. Agencies and programs. Part III. Community organization at work.

HARRIS, OPAL S. A county health department geriatric program. Washington, U.S. Govt. Print. Off., 1961. 13p. (Patterns for progress in aging, case study no. 8.)

Prepared under the direction of the Special Staff on Aging of the U.S. Department of Health, Education, and Welfare. Describes a screening clinic program of diagnostic medical services.

KAPLAN, JEROME. Mobilizing community resources. Chicago, American Public Welfare Association, 1955. 15p. (How public welfare serves aging people, no. 5.)

———— *and others.* An analysis of multiple community services through the institution for the aged. *Geriatrics,* v. 19, October 1964: 773–82.

Sample of 330 aged and chronically ill, involving 2,386 varied contacts.

144

KAPLAN, JEROME, *and others.* Assessing the impact of a gerontological counseling service on community health resources. *Geriatrics,* v. 22, July 1967: 150–154.

Describes an Ohio referral program which resulted in better use of community agencies in planning for the aged and the chronically ill.

KING, CLARENCE. Working with people in community action; an international casebook for trained community workers and voluntary community leaders. New York, Association Press, 1965. 192p.

Realistic examples and actual problems which might help community workers in dealing with people in various communities.

KRAMER, ELAINE, and JOYCE UNGER. A survey of need in a public housing project for the aged. *Gerontologist,* v. 7, September 1967, Pt. I: 204–206; 224.

As a base for community service, the areas of inquiry were: health, retirement, finances, and social life style.

LEEDS, MORTON, ed. Aging in Indiana; readings in community organization. Indianapolis, Ind., State Commission on the Aging and Aged, 1959. 416p.

Emphasizes the mechanics of how to proceed in organizing groups of people to familiarize themselves with the problems of aging.

LEVINE, SOL, *and others.* Community interorganizational problems in providing medical care and social services. *American Journal of Public Health,* v. 53, August 1963: 1183–1195.

Focus on the goals, needs, and problems of individual health and welfare agencies, and how these may impede interorganizational relationships.

MORRIS, ROBERT, ed. Centrally planned change: prospects and concepts. New York, National Association of Social Workers, 1964. 149p.

Analysis of already developed social theory about planned change in welfare, the function of power in American communities, a critique of our existing mechanisms for welfare planning, and the scope of professional responsibility for change.

———— and OLLIE A. RANDALL. Planning and organization of community services for the elderly. *Social Work,* v. 10, January 1965: 96–102.

Effect of the planning structure; factor of civic leadership; relationships between government and voluntary associations; impact of professional styles of action.

NASH, BERNARD E. Community services for the aging. *State Government,* v. 38, Winter 1965: 20–24.

Advocates state programs of consultation in communities to stimulate and strengthen community effort.

NATIONAL COMMISSION ON COMMUNITY HEALTH SERVICES. Health is a community affair. Report. Cambridge, Mass., Harvard University Press, 1966. 252p.
   Appraisal of the personal and environmental health services in the years ahead.

NEW YORK STATE INTERDEPARTMENTAL HEALTH AND HOSPITAL COUNCIL. More than shelter; a guide to the development of community services for the aging in housing projects in New York State. Albany, 1965. 50p.
   Emphasizes services related to housing projects, but is applicable to older persons living elsewhere in the community.

SEMINAR ON COMMUNITY PLANNING FOR OLDER ADULTS. Proceedings of a seminar held at Brandeis University, Waltham, Mass., August 27–September 1, 1961. New York, United Community Funds and Councils of America, Inc., 1962. 111p.
   Purpose of seminar to enlist local leadership to provide continuity and stability in planning for older adults, and to stimulate communities to develop opportunities and services of high quality.

SEMINAR ON STATE-LEVEL PLANNING FOR OLDER PEOPLE. Proceedings. New York, National Council on the Aging, 1964. 95p.
   Practical state-level planning guidelines.

A small town organizes basic services for its aging. *Aging,* no. 109, November 1963: 1–3; 16.
   How Earlham, Iowa, started a community care program for its aged.

STOUGH, ADA BARNETT. A rural county cares for its aging; the story of Aitkin County, Minnesota. Rev. ed. Washington, U.S. Govt. Print. Off., 1967. 24p. (Patterns for progress in aging, case study no. 17.)
   Describes the progress made by the Aitkin County Citizens Committee on Aging.

TRECKER, AUDREY R., and HARLEIGH B. TRECKER. Handbook of community service projects. New York, Association Press, 1960. 519p.
   Section 21 contains 39 projects for older persons.

U.S. ADMINISTRATION ON AGING. "Meeting the challenge of the later years"; guide to community action for Senior Citizens Month 1967 and year-round activity. Washington, 1967. 32p.
   Tool for leaders in aging programs in government, unions, business and professional associations, and private and voluntary organizations.

U.S. BUREAU OF FAMILY SERVICES. Community planning in the public assistance programs. Policies affecting cooperation between public welfare and health and welfare councils. Washington, 1965. 10p.

146

U.S. JOINT TASK FORCE ON HEALTH, EDUCATION, AND WELFARE SERVICES AND HOUSING. Services for families living in public housing; planning for health, education, and welfare services in the public housing community. Washington, U.S. Govt. Print. Off., 1963. 67p.

Deals with major social problems of concern to residents of public housing and offers practical guides for the use and coordination of resources provided through federally aided programs.

U.S. NATIONAL ADVISORY COMMITTEE FOR THE WHITE HOUSE CONFERENCE ON AGING. Background paper on local community organization. Washington, 1960. 68p. (Background paper no. 17.)

Sets forth tested principles, with accompanying illustrative comments, to give guidance to local planning committees.

U.S. PUBLIC HEALTH SERVICE. Comprehensive care services in your community. Washington, U.S. Govt. Print. Off., 1967. 54p. (Public health service publication no. 1353.)

Discusses some of the broad community care service programs developed to meet the diverse needs of ill and disabled patients, with emphasis on the long-term older patient.

U.S. WELFARE ADMINISTRATION. Summary of the Joint Conference on Relationships of Planning Councils and Public Welfare Agencies. Washington, 1965. 37p.

Sponsored by the American Public Welfare Association, National Social Welfare Assembly, United Community Funds and Councils of America, and the Welfare Administration of the U.S. Dept. of Health, Education, and Welfare.

WHITE HOUSE CONFERENCE ON AGING. Local community organization for aging. A report of concerns, considerations, and recommendations with reference to community organization of programs in aging. Washington, U.S. Govt. Print. Off., 1961. 22p. (Reports and guidelines, series no. 12.)

WORKSHOP ON COMMUNITY ACTION TO PROMOTE THE ORAL HEALTH OF THE CHRONICALLY ILL, HANDICAPPED, AND THE AGED. Procedings. Ann Arbor, University of Michigan, School of Public Health, 1965. 156p.

ZALD, MAYER N., ed. Organizing for community welfare. Chicago, Quadrangle, 1967. 316p.

Essays attempt to link findings of sociology with the everyday problems of community welfare.

Homes for the Aged

AMERICAN ASSOCIATION OF HOMES FOR THE AGING. Charitable exemptions for homes for the aging. New York, 1966. 59p.

Historical, philosophical, and legal bases for charitable exemptions of homes for the aged.

AMERICAN ASSOCIATION OF HOMES FOR THE AGING. Directions '67; AAHA conference report no. 5. New York, 1967. 45p.

Edited selections from the 5th annual meeting and conference of the American Association of Homes for the Aging.

————. Focus #2; national and regional issues facing non-profit institutions serving older people, edited selections from AAHA regional institutes. New York, 1966. 46p.

1. National issues. 2. The continuity of care . . . and community planning. 3. The home for the aged and the senior center: areas of mutual interest.

————. The social components of care. New York, 1966. 96p.

BERNSTEIN, LEON. Medicare and the future of homes for the aged. *Journal of Jewish Communal Service,* v. 44, Winter 1967: 192–196.

Suggests impact of Medicare program will correct inadequacies of institutional services in homes for the aged by providing a more comprehensive approach to health care needs.

BRODY, ELAINE M. The impaired aged. A follow-up study of applicants rejected by a voluntary home. *Journal of the American Geriatrics Society,* v. 14, April 1966: 414–420.

Rejection based on staff judgment that more nursing care, supervision, and intensive medical care were needed than could be offered in the facilities then available.

———— and BURTON GUMMER. Aged applicants and non-applicants to a voluntary home: an exploratory comparison. *Gerontologist,* v. 7, December 1967: 234–243.

Study of the case records of the people who request admission and have an in-person interview but don't apply for admission and those who do file.

COHEN, ELIAS S. New patterns and new problems in long-term care. *Professional Nursing Home,* v. 9, April 1967: 34–43.

Discusses problems and forecasts trends and developments of nursing homes and the proprietary home in particular.

COUNCIL OF JEWISH FEDERATIONS AND WELFARE FUNDS. Building and staffing the small home for the aged. New York, 1962. 9p.

Covers cost of construction, operation and staffing of 18 small community sponsored institutions for the aged and chronically sick.

DICK, HARRY R., and HIRAM J. FRIEDSAM. Adjustment of residents of two homes for the aged. *Social Problems,* v. 11, Winter 1964: 282–290.

Analyzes certain aspects of the process of institutionalization as they relate to adjustment while in the home.

FEIL, NAOMI W. Group therapy in a home for the aged. *Gerontologist,* v. 7, September 1967, Pt. I: 192–195.

Focus on residents who cannot fit into the social milieu.

HAMMERMAN, JEROME, and HERBERT SHORE. Value, rationale, use, and implications of a classification system for residents in a home for the aged. *Gerontologist,* v. 4, September 1964, Pt. I: 141–148.

HARRISON, WALTER R. A new look at homes for the aging. *Lutheran Social Welfare Quarterly,* v. 6, December 1966; 32–38.
Indicates new directions for services to the aging.

JONES, LEROY H. Developing a realistic plan for payment of care in a home for the aged. *Lutheran Social Welfare Quarterly,* v. 6, March 1966: 39–44.
Cost based on services or accommodations provided.

KAPLAN, JEROME. Multiple geriatric community services. *Catholic Charities Review,* v. 49, April 1965: 4–12.
Shows how a home for the aged can go beyond its usual residential care program.

KORNZWEIG, A. L. Eye health needs of persons in an institution for the aged. *Sight-Saving Review,* v. 34, Summer 1964: 83–87.
Describes eye clinic at New York City's Jewish Home and Hospital for the Aged.

KURTZ, RUSSELL H., ed. Manual for homes for the aged. New York, Federation of Protestant Welfare Agencies, 1965. Various paging.

LARSON, LAWRENCE E. Isabella Home—a case study of a home for the aged. *Lutheran Social Welfare Quarterly,* v. 3, March 1963: 26–34.
Experience of an institution as it underwent change in program and facilities.

LEEDS, MORTON, and HERBERT SHORE, eds. Geriatric institutional management. New York, Putnam, 1964. 445p.
Focus on the human values in geriatric institutional care, rather than on the technical aspects of institutional management.

NATIONAL ASSOCIATION OF JEWISH HOMES FOR THE AGED. Directory of Jewish homes for the aged in United States and Canada. 3rd ed. Dallas, Texas, 1967. 128p.
Includes summarized information from questionnaires concerning licensure, accreditation, financial arrangements, staff, social services, leisure time programs, medical facilities, average age of residents, building programs, and board of directors.

NATIONAL CONFERENCE OF CATHOLIC CHARITIES. Guides for Catholic homes for the aging. Washington, 1964. 109p.
Defines and characterizes the purposes and guiding policies, suggests steps in planning, and describes services and duties of staff members.

NATIONAL COUNCIL OF SOCIAL SERVICE. COMMITTEE OF ENQUIRY. Caring for people; staffing residential homes. Report. London, Allen & Unwin, 1967. 222p.

> Analyzes problems of the staffs in old people's homes, approved schools, and hostels for the handicapped.

NELSON, GEORGE W. The church home for the aged: where is it headed? *Professional Nursing Home*, v. 9, October 1967: 13–16.

> Reviews six types of facilities for the aged, predicts demise of the proprietary home and tells why the church home has a future.

RANDALL, OLLIE. A modern home for the aging—a community social agency. *Lutheran Social Welfare Quarterly*, v. 5, December 1965: 85–91.

> Discusses national trends and community services.

REINGOLD, JACOB, and ROSE DOBROF. Organization theory and homes for the aged. *Gerontologist*, v. 5, June 1965: 88–95; 112.

ROSEN, THEODORE. The small home for Jewish aged and community service resources. *Journal of Jewish Communal Service*, v. 41, Summer 1965: 384–392.

> Classifies community service resources under those brought into the home for the aged and those used outside at their source.

ROSENBLATT, DANIEL, and IRENE TAVISS. The home for the aged—theory and practice. *Gerontologist*, v. 6, September 1966, Pt. I: 165–168.

> Sets forth two theories which deal with aging and total institutions and discusses these theories in the light of some empirical work which took place within a home for the aged.

SCHULMAN, PHILIP M. Role of the medical coordinator in a home and hospital for the aged. *Journal of the American Geriatrics Society*, v. 12, May 1964: 484–488.

> Outlines the duties of a medical coordinator.

TOWNSEND, PETER. The last refuge; a survey of residential institutions and homes for the aged in England and Wales. London, Routledge and Kegan Paul, 1962. 552p.

> Recent developments in institutional care, types of institutional life, and need for institutional care.

TURNER, HELEN, *and others*. Programs for the mentally impaired in homes for the aged. *Gerontologist*, September 1967, Pt. I: 161–163; 224.

> Discusses homes' recognition of impaired aged persons, presence of a staff psychiatrist, and policies of admission or retention of mentally impaired persons.

150

WOLK, ROBERT L., *and others*. Unique influences and goals of an occupational therapy program in a home for the aged. *Journal of the American Geriatrics Society*, v. 13, November 1965: 989–997.

Discusses the aims and specific projects of the geriatric occupational therapy program of the Menorah Home and Hospital for the Aged and Infirm.

WORKSHOP ON THE RELATIONSHIPS BETWEEN HOSPITALS AND HOMES FOR THE AGED. Proceedings. Chicago, American Hospital Association, 1963. 55p.

Discusses essential coordination of services and continuity of care.

ZELDITCH, MORRIS, and HOWARD B. BRAM. The modern home for the aged; principles underlying design of program and plant. *Gerontologist*, v. 5, June 1965: 67–73.

Discusses homes for the aged supported by voluntary contributions or tax funds.

Housing and Living Arrangements

ANDREWS, R. B. Housing for the elderly. *Gerontologist*, v. 3, September 1963: 110–116; December 1963: 148–151.

Two papers. Subtitle of first paper, "Aspects of its general problem"; second paper, "State and city-county based market analysis, an outline of method and administration."

Architecture for the aging. *Professional Nursing Home*, v. 6, April 1964: 22–68.

Floor plans, layouts, photos from some of the nation's leading architects of nursing homes and homes for the aging.

BEYER, GLENN H. Housing and society. New York, Macmillan, 1965. 595p.

Chapter 13. Housing of the aged.

———— and F. H. J. NIERSTRASZ. Housing the aged in Western countries; programs, dwellings, homes and geriatric facilities. New York, American Elsevier, 1967. 261p.

A comparative examination.

———— and MARGARET E. WOODS. Living and activity patterns of the aged. Ithaca, N.Y., Cornell University, Center for Housing and Environmental Studies, 1963. 29p. (Research report no. 6.)

Focuses on the characteristics of the elderly and their activities which have implications for maintaining independent living arrangements.

CONFERENCE ON THE ROLE OF THE VOLUNTARY AGENCY IN HOUSING FOR THE AGED. The role of the voluntary agency in housing for the aged; conference held at Carnegie International Center, December 9, 1962. New York, Central Bureau for the Jewish Aged, 1963. 32p.

The role of government, by *Marie C. McGuire.* Suitable living arrangements for older people—whose responsibility? by *Beverly Diamond.* Report of work group discussion.

CORNELL UNIVERSITY. HOUSING RESEARCH CENTER. Housing requirements of the aged; a study of design criteria. Ithaca, N.Y., 1958. 124p.

Study prepared for the New York State Division of Housing.

DIAMOND, BEVERLY, ed. Furniture requirements for older people. New York, NCOA Press, 1963. 46p.

Prepared from papers and discussions presented at the first Consumer Institute of the National Council on the Aging.

DICK, HARRY R., *and others.* Residential patterns of aged persons prior to institutionalization. *Journal of Marriage and the Family,* v. 26.

Study of the residential mobility and living arrangements of residents of two voluntary non-profit homes for the aged for 15 years prior to their entrance into the homes.

DONAHUE, WILMA T., ed. Housing the aging. Ann Arbor, University of Michigan Press, 1954. 280p.

Report of the University of Michigan's fifth annual conference on aging.

"Experience reports" on housing for the elderly. *Journal of Housing,* v. 22, July 1965: 352–359.

Report from Minneapolis for the best in design; report from Providence on the best location for a community room; report from Seattle on "pre-testing" design and facilities; report from New York on tenant selection criteria; report from Chicago on variety of design.

FRIEDSAM, HIRAM J., and HARRY R. DICK. Decisions leading to institutionalization of the aged. Denton, Tex., Dept. of Economics and Sociology, North Texas State University, 1963. 64p.

Final report on a project sponsored by the Social Security Administration Cooperative Research and Demonstration Grant Program.

GOETZ, HELEN M. Housekeeping problems of the older homemaker. *Gerontologist,* v. 5, September 1965, Pt. I: 122–124; 159.

Results of an interview with homemakers aged 60–89 years covering activities in the areas of food management, house maintenance, laundry, and personal care.

GOLDSTEIN, SIDNEY. Residential displacement and resettlement of the aged; a study of problems of rehousing aged residents displaced by freeway construction in downtown Providence. Providence, Rhode Island Division on Aging, 1960. 73p.

GRIER, GEORGE W., ed. Housing the aging: research needs. Washington, Brookings Institution, 1962. 413p.

Study prepared for the Housing and Home Finance Agency by the Committee on Problems of the American Community of the Brookings Institution.

INSTITUTE ON MANAGEMENT OF PUBLIC HOUSING FOR THE ELDERLY. Proceedings . . . Toledo, Ohio, Toledo University, 1966. 67p.

Papers and panel discussions include: physical and psychological characteristics of the elderly; social problems of aging; management policies and practices in housing the elderly; welfare services; neighborhood centers; health services.

INTERFAITH CONFERENCE ON HOUSING FOR SENIOR CITIZENS. Proceedings. Washington, U.S. Housing and Home Finance Agency, Office of the Administrator, Office of Housing for Senior Citizens, 1966. 75p.

Major statements and reports.

ISENSTADT, THEODORE R. Changing social orientation of the Jewish aged—a profile. *Journal of Jewish Communal Service.* v. 41, Fall 1964: 124–131.

More services should be offered to enable the older person to live independently in the community.

————. Programs and services that enable the aging person to remain in the comunity. *Lutheran Social Welfare Quarterly,* v. 4, September 1964: 53–59.

Discusses major aids to enable older people to be sustained in their homes and in the community.

JOYCE, DAVID, *and others.* The social functioning of the dislodged elderly; a study of post-relocation assistance. Philadelphia, Institute for Environmental Studies, University of Pennsylvania, 1966. 89p.

Focus on ways to overcome difficulties faced by elderly people in re-establishing social ties in a new neighborhood after relocation.

LAGING, BARBARA. Furniture design for the elderly. *Rehabilitation Literature,* v. 27, May 1966: 130–140.

Results of a survey of some of the solutions to the furniture needs of the elderly person that have been developed in the U.S. and Europe in the past few years.

LANGFORD, MARILYN. Community aspects of housing for the aged. Ithaca, N.Y., Cornell University, 1962. 49p. (Center for housing and environmental studies, research report no. 5.)

MUSE, MARIANNE. Homes for old age. *Journal of Home Economics,* v. 57, March 1965: 183–187.

Comparisons of the plans of couples 50 to 64 years of age for homes for their later years with the actual living arrangements of couples, widows, and widowers age 65 or older.

MUSSON, NOVERE, and HELEN HEUSINKVELD. Buildings for the elderly. New York, Reinhold, 1963. 216p.

> Examines the kinds of residences for older people now available and popular, looks at the kinds of residences now being planned, and evaluates current concepts.

NATIONAL ASSOCIATION OF HOUSING AND REDEVELOPMENT OFFICIALS. Management of public housing for the elderly; background readings. Washington, 1965. 92p.

> Results from a management training program to develop a set of materials which provide an introduction to the characteristics of the low-income elderly for housing management staff.

NATIONAL COUNCIL ON THE AGING. Building for older people—financing, location, construction, administration. New York, 1961. Various paging.

> Based on proceedings of two conferences. Part 1—The Seminar on Housing and Living Arrangements for the Later Years (June 1960); part 2—The Institute on Producing Housing for Older People (March 1961).

NEW YORK UNIVERSITY. GRADUATE SCHOOL OF PUBLIC ADMINISTRATION. Management of public housing for the elderly. New York, 1963. 2v.

> Part 1, by *Troy R. Westmeyer.* Part 2, by *Max Franc,* has subtitle, Built-in aids to management.

NEWCOMB, DUANE G. Mobile homes that grow and grow. *Harvest Years,* v. 6, March 1966: 4–11.

> Detailed information about expanding homes or homes with expanding rooms.

NIEBANCK, PAUL L., and JOHN B. POPE. The elderly in older urban areas; problems of adaptation and the effects of relocation. Philadelphia, Institute for Environmental Studies, University of Pennsylvania, 1965. 174p.

> Characteristics of elderly residents being relocated and the general impact of relocation, and programs being used or which might be used to improve the relocation process.

PENNSYLVANIA UNIVERSITY INSTITUTE FOR URBAN STUDIES. Essays on the problems faced in the relocation of elderly persons. 2d ed. Philadelphia, 1964. 137p.

> Study sponsored by the Ford Foundation and carried out by the Institute for Urban Studies of the University of Pennsylvania and the National Association of Housing and Redevelopment Officials to develop more adequate means of easing the burden relocation places on the elderly.

154

PETTIT, LOIS. Aged and alone in Detroit, a service study of the health and welfare needs of aged persons who live alone in the central part of Detroit. Detroit, Neighborhood Service Organization, 1961. 4v.

Part I. The aged in Jefferies homes. Part II. The aged in downtown hotels and rooming houses. Part III. The aged in homes which they own or are owned by their adult children. Part IV. Summary.

PHILLIPS, BERNARD S. The aging in a central Illinois community. Urbana, Illinois, Small Homes Council—Building Research Council, 1962. 101p.

Survey of aging in Decatur, Ill., proposed by the city of Decatur and conducted under the auspices of the University of Illinois Council on Community Development with the support of the city of Decatur, the University Research Board, and the Department of Sociology.

REICH, JULIE M., and others. Relocating the dispossessed elderly; a study of Mexican-Americans. Philadelphia, Institute for Environmental Studies, University of Pennsylvania, 1966. 136p.

The welfare of elderly persons of ethnic minorities, and the problems in communication among agencies in aiding these persons when faced with relocation.

RESEARCH CONFERENCE ON PATTERNS OF LIVING AND HOUSING OF THE MIDDLE-AGED AND OLDER PEOPLE. Proceedings. Washington, U.S. Govt. Print. Off., 1966. 181p. (Public Health Service publication no. 1496.)

RICCITELLI, M. L. Modern housing programs for the elderly in Connecticut. *Journal of the American Geriatrics Society,* v. 12, August 1964: 756–762.

U.S. BUREAU OF THE CENSUS. 1960 census of housing. Washington, U.S. Govt. Print. Off.

Vol. VII. Housing of senior citizens; United States, States, selected metropolitan areas. Characteristics of persons 60 years old and over and the housing units and households in which they live.

U.S. CONGRESS. SENATE. COMMITTEE ON LABOR AND PUBLIC WELFARE. Aging Americans, their views and living conditions. Washington, U.S. Govt. Print. Off., 1961. 52p. (86th Cong., 2d sess., committee print.)

Problems of the aged as told by the elderly themselves at townhall sessions and as observed at the facilities for senior citizens.

————. ————. SPECIAL COMMITTEE ON AGING. Housing for the elderly. Washington, U.S. Govt. Print. Off., 1962. 57p. (87th Cong., 2d sess., committee print.)

Conclusions and recommendations based on an examination of the scope and magnitude of housing problems of older citizens and current governmental and private efforts to meet these problems.

155

U.S. FEDERAL HOUSING ADMINISTRATION. Minimum property standards; housing for the elderly, with special consideration for the handicapped. Washington, 1967. 117p.

Apply to properties submitted for mortgage insurance under various sections of the National Housing Act, and are confined in their application to the individual property within its property lines.

U.S. NATIONAL ADVISORY COMMITTEE FOR THE WHITE HOUSE CONFERENCE ON AGING. Background paper on housing. Washington, U.S. Govt. Print. Off., 1960. 73p. (Background paper no. 8.)

Retirement Communities

BARKER, MICHAEL B. California retirement communities. Berkeley, Calif., Center for Real Estate and Urban Economics, Institute of Urban and Regional Development, University of California, 1966. 103p. (Special report 2.)

How a retirement community is organized, its relationship to the municipal corporation, and an analysis of two retirement communities.

BLANCHARD, FESSENDEN S. Make the most of your retirement; where to go, what to do, how much it costs. Garden City, N.Y., Doubleday, 1963. 340p.

Advice and information for those about to retire or those who already have.

BURGESS, ERNEST W., ed. Retirement villages. Ann Arbor, University of Michigan, Division of Gerontology, 1961. 156p.

Describes location and design, operation and services, and financing. Gives alternatives and perspectives of communities whose residents are mainly older people.

CARP, FRANCES MERCHANT. A future for the aged; Victoria Plaza and its residents. Austin, Tex., University of Texas Press, 1966. 287p.

Report of a high-rise public housing facility for low-income elderly people in San Antonio, Texas.

CIUCA, AL. A new form of assistance for aged people of the rural milieu; the old people's village. *Geriatrics,* v. 20, December 1965: 1070–1074.

Experimental settlement for old people in Rumania, with surroundings and living conditions similar to those to which they have been accustomed.

CONNECTICUT. JOINT STUDY COMMISSION OF THE COMMISSION ON SERVICES FOR ELDERLY PERSONS AND PUBLIC WORKS DEPT. Report on feasibility and costs of developing a model mobile home park to be occupied by retired persons and their spouses. Hartford, 1966. 30p.

FORD, NORMAN D. Retirement hotels roll out the red carpet. *Harvest Years*, v. 5, December 1965: 4–11.
Describes hotels with clublike facilities and nursing-home care, and includes a directory of retirement hotels.

FRUSH, JAMES, JR., and BENSON ESCHENBACH. The retirement residence; an analysis of the architecture and management of life-care housing. Springfield, Ill., Thomas, 1968. 108p.
Examines the problem within an economic framework.

HEUSINKVELD, HELEN, and NOVERRE MUSSON. 1001 best places to live when you retire. Chicago, Dartnell Corporation, 1964. 160p.
Directory of alphabetical listings by city and residence name under each state name, of over 1500 retirement residences.

LAMBERT, EDOUARD. Reflections on a policy for retirement. *International Labour Review*, v. 90, October 1964: 365–375.
General discussion on retirement and the fundamental criteria to be met by schemes of income maintenance and housing for older people, and main features of a French retirement village.

NATIONAL COUNCIL ON THE AGING. A national directory on housing for older people, including a guide for selection. New York, 1965. 222p.

PARKER, W. RUSSELL. Multi-unit retirement housing for rural areas; a guide to design considerations for architects, engineers, and builders. Washington, U.S. Govt. Print. Off., 1965. 23p. (Agriculture information bulletin no. 297.)

REMMLEIN, MADALINE KINTNER. Housing for the retired teacher, a planning guide. Washington, National Education Association, 1962. 82p.
Handbook for education associations sponsoring the planning and construction of apartments, houses, and colonies for retired teachers.

SAN DIEGO. PLANNING DEPT. Retirement housing: a planning analysis. San Diego, Calif., 1966. 135p.
Current and likely future impact of senior citizen housing developments in the community, with specific recommendations to assist public and private enterprise in planning for this housing.

SMITH, MARTHA LIGON. Foreign retirement edens. San Antonio, Tex., Naylor, 1967. 88p.
Case histories and facts of life about life in a foreign colony.

STROMME, GEORGE, ed. Resort-retirement facilities register. San Francisco, Drake Publications, 1967. 4v.
Published in geographic sections: 1. California; 2. Northwestern; 3. Southern; 4. Northeastern.

WALKLEY, ROSABELLE PRICE, *and others.* Retirement housing in California. Berkeley, Calif., Diablo Press, 1966. 134p.

Status of construction, site locations, sponsorship, costs and financial arangements, and programs and services available.

Senior Centers

CUMMINGS, MILTON C., *and others.* Adventures in learning, frontiers past 60 in Hamilton, Ohio. A Study of Hamilton's center for older people. Washington, U.S. Govt. Print. Off., 1961. 32p. (Office of education bulletin 1961, no. 13.)

FRANKEL, GODFREY. The multi-purpose senior citizens' center: a new comprehensive agency. *Gerontologist,* v. 6, March 1966: 23–27.

Background and description of the multi-purpose senior citizens' center.

MCCARTHY, HENRY L. Day centers for older people. Chicago, American Public Welfare Association, 1954. 15p. (How public welfare serves aging people, no. 4.)

MAXWELL, JEAN M. Centers for older people; guide for programs and facilities. New York, National Council on Aging, 1962. 118p.

———— and ALICE ADLER, eds. Tomorrow's centers; a symposium of papers. New York, NCOA Press, 1963. 60p.

Exploratory conference organized by the National Council on the Aging.

NATIONAL CONFERENCE OF SENIOR CENTERS. Proceedings, New York, National Council on the Aging.

Each annual meeting has a distinctive theme.

NATIONAL CONFERENCE ON SOCIAL WELFARE. The multi-purpose center for older people; new focal point for social services, social planning and action. New York, National Council on the Aging, 1966. 32p.

Three papers relating to the expanded role of senior centers.

NATIONAL COUNCIL ON THE AGING. Centers for older people; guide for programs and facilities. New York, 1962. 118p.

Report on a two-year project.

SCHRAMM, WILBUR LANG, and ERNEST R. HILGARD. Little House, a study of senior citizens. Menlo Park, Calif., Peninsula Volunteers, 1961. 351p.

TRYON, ARTHUR H. A senior citizens service center. Washington, U.S. Govt. Print. Off., 1961. 18p. (Patterns for progress in aging, case study no. 10.)

Report on the Los Angeles County Senior Citizens Service Center.

TUCKMAN, JACOB. Factors related to attendance in a center for older people. *Journal of the American Geriatrics Society,* v. 15, May 1967: 474–479.

Analysis of attendance records over a three-month period showed good health and living relatively close to a clinically-oriented center for older people were the only factors related to greater frequency of attendance.

U.S. ADMINISTRATION ON AGING. National directory of senior centers. Washington, U.S. Govt. Print. Off., 1966. 201p.

Issued in cooperation with the National Council on the Aging and the President's Council on Aging.

VICKERY, FLORENCE E. A multi-service senior center—its unique role and function. *Gerontologist,* v. 5, December 1965: 246–277.

Describes programs and procedures of the San Francisco Senior Center.

Social Services and Social Work

AMERICAN PUBLIC WELFARE ASSOCIATION. COMMITTEE ON AGING. Aging . . . public welfare's role. Social service needs of older people and the role of public welfare in meeting these needs. Chicago, 1960. 20p.

Policy statement adopted by the board of directors of the APWA in February 1960.

———. PUBLIC WELFARE PROJECT ON AGING. The homemaker in public welfare. Chicago, 1962. 32p.

Four papers were presented at APWA's 1961 National biennial conference at a session titled "Home maker services—prop to strengthen family life."

———. ———. Medical care for the aging; casework services in public welfare agencies. Chicago, 1963. 40p.

Report of an institute held Nov. 19–20, 1962.

———. ———. Potentials for service through group work in public welfare. Chicago, 1962. 28p.

Three papers describing ways in which social group work is being utilized to help older people.

ANDERSON, JAMES V. Social work services in a residential institution for the aged. *Lutheran Social Welfare Quarterly,* v. 1, Spring 1967: 54–62.

Nature and function of a residential institution for the aged, and specific elements which may be included in the social services.

BASS, BERNICE E., and JOSEPH C. MATCHAR. Group counseling: experiences with aging men in an out-patient department. *Journal of the American Geriatrics Society,* v. 13, July 1965: 687–693.

Presents the objectives and goals of a group counseling program and the techniques used in approaching these goals.

BECKER, DOROTHY G. Casework for the aged poor: a renewed drive for public-voluntary teamwork. *Social Casework*, v. 47, May 1966: 293–301.

Describes a demonstration project on services to the aged.

BLENKNER, MARGARET, *and others*. Protective services for older people: final report on the planning phase of a research and demonstration project. Cleveland, Benjamin Rose Institute, 1964. 39p.

————, ————. Serving the aging; an experiment in social work and public health nursing. New York, Community Service Society of New York, 1964. 249p.

Study extending over an eight-year period from 1955 through 1962.

BURR, JAMES J. Protective services for older persons. Washington, U.S. Govt. Print. Off., 1964. 36p. (P. A. report no. 54.)

A guide for public welfare planning put out by the U.S. Bureau of Family Services.

BUTTS, SARAH A. Casework services in public assistance medical care. Washington, U.S. Govt. Print. Off., 1962. 110p.

Directed to the more common illnesses and related social needs of patients who are neither mentally ill nor receiving care in nursing homes and rehabilitation settings.

————. Medical deprivation and social services. *Public Welfare*, v. 44, January 1966: 79–82; 90–91.

Stresses importance of the caseworker in helping clients to use medical services.

BYRON, EVELYN S. A friendly visiting program. Washington, U.S. Govt. Print. Off., 1961. 16p. (Patterns for progress in aging, case study no. 13.)

Study of the programs developed by the Volunteer Bureau of the Metropolitan Welfare Council of Chicago.

CAIN, LILLIAN PIKE, and DORIS W. EPSTEIN. The utilization of housewives as volunteer case aides. *Social Casework*, v. 48, May 1967: 282–285.

Describes characteristics of the aides, the structure of the program and its operation.

CENTRAL BUREAU FOR THE JEWISH AGED. Dynamic factors in the role of the caseworker in work with the aged. New York, 1962. 62p.

Proceedings of the *Institute on Casework Service with the Aged* held October 19, 1961, at the Carnegie Endowment Center.

COHEN, NATHAN E., ed. The citizen volunteer; his responsibility, role, and opportunity in modern society. New York, Harper, 1960. 276p.

Chapter 13. "Volunteers in programs for the older citizen," by *Louis Lowy*.

COMMUNITY COUNCIL OF GREATER NEW YORK. BUDGET STANDARD SERV-
ICE. RESEARCH DEPARTMENT. How to measure ability to pay for
social and health services. Rev. ed. New York, 1967. 39p.
   Manual outlining procedures which may be used at arriving at
   equitable fees.

CUMMING, ROGER J. Growing problems in protective services for the
aged. *Geriatrics,* v. 21, September 1966: 163–173.
   Physicians should recognize and assess a patient's need for socio-
   economic as well as medical help and be able to bring it to the
   patient.

EDGE, J. R., and I. D. M. NELSON. Survey of arrangements for the
elderly in Barrow-in-Furness. *Medical Care,* v. 1, October-December
1963: 202–218.
   Study of the medical and social circumstances of all elderly people
   in hospitals and a sample of those in the community as a basis
   on which to assess need for medical and welfare services.

ELDER, RUTH N. What is a normal older person? *Lutheran Social Welfare Quarterly,* v. 6, December 1966: 39–50.
   Material presented in the context of "The Disengagement Theory"
   for services to the aged.

FARRAR, MARCELLA, and MARY L. HEMMY. Use of nonprofessional staff
in work with the aged. *Social work,* v. 8, July 1963: 44–50.
   Describes an experiment at the Benjamin Rose Institute.

——— *and others.* Social work responsibility in nursing home care.
Social Casework, v. 45, November 1964: 527–533.
   The role of the social worker in placing older people in nursing
   homes.

FILKER, DAVID. Employing young mothers to assist the elderly: Baltimore housing agency experiments with young-old mutual aid program. *Journal of Housing,* v. 23, December 1966: 650–653.
   Pilot program that brings together tenant groups in a neighbor-
   to-neighbor job training and assistance project.

FORD, CAROLINE S. Ego-adaptive mechanisms of older persons. *Social
Casework,* v. 46, January 1965: 16–21.
   Discusses the three major stress areas for the aged: the social, the
   physical, and the emotional.

FORMAN, MARK, and EVELYN MARON. Developing a casework service to
older adults in a group work setting. *Journal of Jewish Communal
Service,* v. 43, Summer 1967: 312–317.
   Describes a joint project of the Wilmington Jewish Community
   Center and the Jewish Family Service of Northern Delaware.

161

HALL, GERTRUDE H., ed. The law and the impaired older person: protection or punishment? New York, National Council on the Aging, 1966. 51p.

Panel discussion of an actual legal case pointing out the importance of protecting the individual rights of an impaired older person.

HANDY, IMENA A. Fifty aging men: a demonstration project in social services to psychiatric geriatric patients. *Journal of the American Geriatrics Society*, v. 15, March 1967: 295–301.

HANSON, MILTON C. The casework process in work with the aged. *Lutheran Social Welfare Quarterly*, v. 6, March 1966: 3–14.

Steps involved in the casework process through the use of theoretical material and a case presentation.

INSTITUTE ON PROVISION OF SOCIAL SERVICES FOR NURSING HOME PATIENTS. Proceedings. Washington, U.S. Public Health Service, 1965. 81p.

Emerging patterns of consultation to nursing homes and their implications to social workers.

Issue on aging. *Lutheran Social Welfare Quarterly*, v. 4, September 1964: entire issue.

Underlying philosophy of aging, skills and patterns necessary for appropriate service, need for sound planning of services.

KAPLAN, JEROME, and GORDON J. ALDRIDGE, eds. Social welfare of the aging. New York, Columbia University Press, 1962. 372p. (Aging around the world, vol. 2.)

Proceedings of the fifth congress of the *International Association of Gerontology*. Five major topics: institutional care and planning; leisure-time activities; community organization; social aspects of medicine; and counseling, casework, and social service.

———— *and others.* An analysis of multiple community services through the institution for the aged. *Geriatrics*, v. 19, October 1964: 773–782.

The effect social service has in returning people to various degrees of self-care and independent living and in insuring the maintenance of this self-care.

KELLAM, CONSTANCE E., and CHARLES T. O'REILLY. Measuring the needs of older people. Madison, School of Social Work, University of Wisconsin, 1964. Various paging.

Analysis of the findings of a group of caseworkers in 20 counties of 6 states in 1962.

KIMMEL, DOROTHY G. Homemaker service for older people. Chicago, American Public Welfare Association, 1955. 15p. (How public welfare serves aging people, no. 6.)

LARSON, NEOTA. Protective services for older adults. *Public Welfare,* v. 22, October 1964: 247–251; 276.

Concentrates on the problems of older persons in the social security system.

LEACH, JEAN M. The intergenerational approach in casework with the aging. *Social Casework,* v. 45, March 1964: 144–149.

Based on the experiences of ten caseworkers in a family agency and the insights that emerged in their attempt to deepen their understanding of the emotional forces that affect the lives of aging clients.

LEEDS, MORTON. The aged, the social worker, and the community. Cleveland, Howard Allen, 1961. 114p.

Treats the inter-relationships of the professional social worker and the various agencies working in the field of aging.

LOEB, MARTIN B., *and others.* Norms of rural aged and welfare tasks. *Gerontologist,* v. 5, September 1965, Part I: 118–124.

Norms of adaptive patterns to identify social work tasks in facilitating the adjustment between the older person and his environment.

LOWY, LOUIS. Roadblocks in group work practice with older people: a framework for analysis. *Gerontologist,* v. 7, June 1967, Pt. I: 109–113; 135.

MANNING, HELEN C. More than bread; social services in public assistance . . . a community resource. Washington, U.S. Govt. Print. Off., 1958. 24p.

Prepared for use of community leaders, members of civic groups, and other interested citizens to show what social services in public assistance are and what they do to help people solve their difficulties.

MARGULIES, MARTIN S. Classification of activities to meet the psychosocial needs of geriatric patients. *Gerontologist,* v. 6, December 1966: 207–211.

Meeting the psycho-social needs of the institutionalized aged through group work processes.

MILLOY, MARGARET. Casework with the older person and his family. *Social Casework,* v. 45, October 1964: 450–456.

Diagnostic considerations related to ways of helping older people and their families.

MONTELIUS, MARJORIE. Working with groups: a guide for administration of group services in public welfare. Washington, U.S. Govt. Print. Off., 1966. 57p.

Identifies certain areas of concern and attempts to answer questions raised about the process of working with people in groups.

MORTON, MALVIN, ed. Chronic disease; a handbook for public welfare workers. Chicago, American Public Welfare Association, 1966. 63p.
Supplement to *Public Welfare,* October 1966.

NATIONAL ASSOCIATION OF SOCIAL WORKERS. Encyclopedia of social work; successor to the social work year book. 15th ed. New York, 1965. 1060p.

NATIONAL CONFERENCE ON SOCIAL WELFARE. A crucial issue in social work practice; protective services for older people. New York, National Council on the Aging, 1966. 55p.
Papers by authorities from the legal, medical, and social work fields.

————. The social welfare forum, official proceedings. New York, Columbia University Press.
From 1874 through 1916 called Conference of Charities and Corrections. From 1917 through 1928 called Conference of Social Work. From 1929 through 1956 called National Conference of Social Work.

————. Social work with groups. New York, National Association of Social Workers.
Selected papers from the annual forum. Title varies.

NATIONAL COUNCIL FOR HOMEMAKER SERVICES. Directory of homemaker-home health aide services in the United States and Canada, 1966–67. New York, 1967. 181p.

————. Homemaker-home health aides; training manual. New York, 1967. 181p.
Unit of instruction VII. The ill, the disabled and the aging adult.

NATIONAL COUNCIL ON THE AGING. Guardianship and protective services for older people. New York, 1963. 184p.
Analyzes the realities and trends in handling the problems of older people who cannot, without outside assistance, care for themselves or their assets.

O'NEILL, VIRGINIA. Protecting older people. *Public Welfare,* v. 23, April 1965: 119–127.
Help older people remain in their own homes, in familiar surroundings and close to family.

PEARSE, DOROTHY T. Three years later—an evaluation of volunteer training. *Gerontologist,* v. 6, September 1966, Pt. I: 154–158.
Describes a three-year demonstration project and assesses the results three years later.

164

PETERS, MARY OVERHOLT. Caseworker . . . person with value. Rev. ed. Chicago, American Public Welfare Association, 1967. 34p.
Delineates the service function in public welfare. *The Aged, Too, Need Friends,* p. 25–32.

PINCUS, ALLEN. Toward a developmental view of aging for social work. *Social Work,* v. 12, July 1967: 33–41.
Theoretical orientations by which social work views the aging process and some current research and theory on personality processes in aging.

PUTTER, ZETTA H. Group approaches in the care of the chronically ill. *Journal of Jewish Communal Service,* v. 44, Winter 1967: 177–183.
Describes work with groups of patients once they have left the hospital and are re-established in the community.

RICHARDSON, I. M. Age and need; a study of older people in Northeast Scotland. Edinburgh, E & S Livingstone, 1964. 124p.
Needs and problems of older people and the adequacy of the services available to help them.

RUDD, T. N. Human relations in old age. London, Faber, 1967. 144p.
Handbook for social workers, health visitors and others.

SAFIER, RUTH. Homemakers for chronically ill and aged: a description. *Gerontologist,* v. 6, September 1966, Pt. I: 150–153.
Three prerequisites for staff selection in homemaker service.

SEMINAR ON SOCIAL GROUP WORK WITH OLDER PEOPLE. Proceedings . . . June 5–10, 1961. New York, National Association of Social Workers, 1963. 176p.
Co-sponsored by the American Public Welfare Association, National Council on the Aging, and National Association of Social Workers.

SEMINAR ON THE AGING. Proceedings. New York, Council on Social Work Education, 1959. 2v.
Vol. I. Toward better understanding of the aged. Vol. II. Social work education for better services to the aging.

SMITH, LUCILLE M. Homemaker service: luxury or necessity? *New Outlook for the Blind,* v. 57, November 1963: 337–343.
Past, present, and future of homemaker services in the United States.

STEWART, WILLIAM H., *and others.* Homemaker services in the United States, 1958; a nationwide study. Washington, U.S. Govt. Print. Off., 1958. 92p. (Public Health Service publication no. 644.)
Appendix contains questionnaires sent to: agency providing homemaker services; employee providing direct "home help" service; family served by homemaker during study week.

STRAUSS, GLADYS. The nursing home and the volunteer. *Catholic Charities Review*, v. 48. September 1964: 14–17.

Recommends more youthful volunteers for nursing homes.

SYRACUSE UNIVERSITY. SCHOOL OF SOCIAL WORK. Toward better social work services for the aging; an institute on social and health needs. Syracuse, N.Y., 1960. 62p.

TARPY, ELEANOR K., *and others.* Intensive casework with chronically ill, neuropsychiatric geriatric patients. *Journal of the American Geriatrics Society,* v. 12, November 1964: 1077–1082.

Describes the results; half of the patients were given intensive casework help, and the other half were given the usual casework help available to all patients.

TRAVIS, GEORGIA. Chronic disease and disability. Berkeley, University of California Press, 1961. 295p.

A medical-social guidebook for the use of the nonmedically trained social worker.

TURNER, HELEN. Helping aged persons: casework, a basic service. *Lutheran Social Welfare Quarterly,* v. 4, September 1964: 45–52.

Outlines general casework principles of special importance in their application to work with aged persons, and focuses on a particular way in which the use of casework relationships can make a difference to clients.

U.S. BUREAU OF FAMILY SERVICES. Foster family care for the aged. Washington, U.S. Govt. Print. Off., 1965. 41p. (P. A. report no. 56.)

Surveys possibilities of foster family care and offers suggestions for the most effective development and use of these services.

U.S. CONGRESS. SENATE. SPECIAL COMMITTEE ON AGING. Services for senior citizens—recommendations and comment. Washington, U.S. Govt. Print. Off., 1964. 19p. (88th Cong., 2d sess., report no. 1542.)

Suggests ways in which the federal and local governments can work together in establishing and expanding public and private services.

U.S. NATIONAL ADVISORY COMMITTEE FOR THE WHITE HOUSE CONFERENCE ON AGING. Background paper on national voluntary services and service organizations. Washington, U.S. Govt. Print. Off., 1960. 34p. (Background paper no. 19.)

————. Background paper on social services for the aging. Washington, U.S. Govt. Print. Off., 1960. 70p. (Background paper no. 7.)

WASSER, EDNA, comp. Casebook on work with the aging. New York, Family Service Association, 1966. Various paging.

Ten cases from the Family Service Association of America Project on Aging.

166

WASSER, EDNA, comp. Creative approaches in casework with the aging. New York, Family Service Association, 1966. 98p.

————. Family casework focus on the older person. *Social Casework,* v. 47, July 1966: 423–431.

————. The sense of commitment in serving older persons. *Social Casework,* v. 45, October 1964: 443–449.
Concerned with the social worker's development of knowledge and skills to meet the needs and demands of the older person.

WATKINS, ELIZABETH G. Friendly visitors. Chicago, American Public Welfare Association, 1955. 15p. (How public welfare serves aging people, no. 7.)

WEBBER, IRVING L., ed. Services for the aging. Gainesville, University of Florida Press, 1957. 159p. (Institute of gerontology series no. 7.)
Report on the seventh annual Conference on Gerontology held at the University of Florida, March 14–15, 1957.

WEBER, RUTH E. Older persons in need of protective services encountered by thirteen selected Cleveland agencies in March 1964: a survey. Cleveland, Benjamin Rose Institute, 1964. Various paging.

WELFARE COUNCIL OF METROPOLITAN CHICAGO. Guidelines and goals for group services for the older adult. Chicago, 1965. 21p.
Prepared for individuals or sponsors who wish to start a small program.

WHITE HOUSE CONFERENCE ON AGING. National voluntary services and service organizations in aging. A statement of position, roles, and potentials of national voluntary organizations in the field of aging, together with the policy statement and supporting recommendations on this subject formulated at the 1961 White House Conference on Aging. Washington, U.S. Govt. Print. Off., 1961. 26p. (Reports and guidelines, series no. 14.)

YOUNG, JEANNE G. Meeting the social needs of Medicare patients. *Gerontologist,* v. 7, December 1967: 261–265.
The role of the medical social worker.

Training of Professional Personnel

AMERICAN PUBLIC WELFARE ASSOCIATION. PUBLIC WELFARE PROJECT ON AGING. Strengthening social services for the aging through public welfare staff development. Chicago, 1961. 48p.
Report of an institute held in April 1961.

HAWAII UNIVERSITY. SCHOOL OF PUBLIC HEALTH. GERONTOLOGY CURRICULUM DEVELOPMENT STUDY. A report prepared for the Hawaii State Commission on Aging. Honolulu, 1966. 2v.

V. 1. Education in gerontology for Hawaii. V. 2. Age structure of Hawaii population.

INSTITUTE ON THE SIGNIFICANCE OF MEDICARE: A SYSTEM FOR THE DELIVERY OF COMPREHENSIVE MEDICAL CARE. Proceedings . . . Philadelphia, Home and Hospital for the Jewish Aged of the Philadelphia Geriatric Center, 1967. 123p.

Institute to train health and welfare personnel in the southeastern Pennsylvania region.

INTER-UNIVERSITY TRAINING INSTITUTE IN SOCIAL GERONTOLOGY. Syllabi in social gerontology; a syllabus and annotated bibliography. Ann Arbor, Institute for Social Gerontology, University of Michigan, 1959. 5v.

JACOBS, HENRY LEE. Youth looks at aging; an approach to content for a unit of study on aging at the secondary school level; a teacher's guide for a unit of three or four weeks. Iowa City, University of Iowa, Institute of Gerontology and Division of Extension and University Services, 1964. 41p. (Extension service bulletin no. 819.)

KRAUSS, THEODORE C. The role of geriatrics and gerontology in medical education. *Journal of the American Geriatrics Society,* v. 13, August 1965: 699–707.

Reasons why geriatrics and gerontology should be stressed as an important part of the total medical curriculum.

KUSHNER, ROSE E., and MARION E. BUNCH, eds. Graduate education in aging within the social sciences. Ann Arbor, Mich., Division of Gerontology, University of Michigan, 1967. 118p.

Guidelines to aid universities and other training institutions in planning and organizing graduate programs of education in social gerontology.

MEYER, CAROL H. Staff development in public welfare agencies. New York, Columbia University Press, 1966. 230p.

Problem of equipping available civil service personnel to meet the need for social services.

MICKEY, CARROL M. A curriculum in social gerontology for those interested in health care for the aged. Washington, Dept. of Health Care Administration, George Washington University, 1967. 155p.

Intended to provide a curriculum in social gerontology directly applicable to a graduate-level program in the administration of long-term care, and adaptable to educational progress in other related fields.

SPEAR, MEL. New program expectations in serving the aged. *Public Welfare*, v. 24, July 1966: 211–217.

Report on a project for utilizing in-service training of staff as a principal vehicle for improving public welfare services for aged persons.

TANNAR, VIRGINIA L. Selected social work concepts for public welfare workers. Washington, U.S. Govt. Print. Off., 1964. 150p.

Designed by the U.S. Bureau of Family Services to help public welfare agencies in the development of skilled personnel.

TIBBITTS, CLARK, and WILMA DONAHUE, eds. Aging in today's society. Englewood Cliffs, N.J., Prentice-Hall, 1960. 418p.

Expansion and revision of "Aging in the modern world," published in 1957 by the Fund for Adult Education for the purpose of stimulating group study and discussion of the materials and problems it was concerned with.

TRAINING INSTITUTE FOR PUBLIC WELFARE SPECIALISTS ON AGING. Planning welfare services for older people. Washington, U.S. Govt. Print. Off., 1966. 198p.

Collection of papers from a training institute for public welfare officials from states and communities.

U.S. BUREAU OF FAMILY SERVICES. Characteristics of staff development provisions in state public assistance and child welfare services plans under the Social Security Act. Washington, U.S. Govt. Print. Off., 1965. 160p. (Public assistance report no. 51.)

Provisions include orientation, in-service training, and professional education for all personnel.

U.S. NATIONAL ADVISORY COMMITTEE FOR THE WHITE HOUSE CONFERENCE ON AGING. Background paper on education for aging. Washington, U.S. Govt. Print. Off., 1960. 146p. (Background paper no. 9.)

————. Background paper on role and training of professional personnel. Washington, U.S. Govt. Print. Off., 1960. 147p. (Background paper no. 10.)

U.S. OFFICE OF AGING. DIVISION OF RESEARCH AND TRAINING. Training in social gerontology and its application, a suggested university curriculum. Washington, U.S. Govt. Print. Off., 1965. 21p. (OA no. 222.)

WHITE HOUSE CONFERENCE ON AGING. Education for aging. A report of the problems and issues together with the recommendations and policy statements from the White House Conference on Aging. Washington, U.S. Govt. Print. Off., 1961. 41p. (Reports and guidelines, series no. 2.)

————. The role and training of professional personnel in the field of aging. A statement of needs, approaches, and programs together with recommendations from the 1961 White House Conference on Aging. Washington, U.S. Govt. Print. Off., 1961. 58p. (Reports and guidelines, series no. 8.)

AUTHOR INDEX

N

180

181

183

SUBJECT
INDEX